The Counter-R
Franc
1787–1830

THE COUNTER-REVOLUTION IN FRANCE 1787–1830

James Roberts

MACMILLAN

First published 1990

Published by
MACMILLAN EDUCATION LTD
Houndmills, Basingstoke, Hampshire RG21 2XS
and London
Companies and representatives
throughout the world

Printed in Hong Kong

British Library Cataloguing in Publication Data
Roberts, James
The counter-revolution in France 1787–1830.
1. France. Political events, history
I. Title
944
ISBN 0–333–48318–9
ISBN 0–333–48319–7 pbk

Contents

Preface

The Counter-Revolution is no longer regarded as an awkward footnote to the history of the Revolution itself. The most recent general work on the Revolution, for example, by D. M. G. Sutherland, is titled *Revolution and Counter-Revolution*. This, of course, is a much more accurate label for a period which is not fully comprehensible except in terms of the conflict between the two movements. It is a conflict which also forms in many ways the central theme of much of the recent past: the history of both France and Europe in the nineteenth and twentieth centuries reflects the counter-revolutionary as much as the revolutionary tradition. The Counter-Revolution was more than simply the rejection of the Revolution although it was, of course, that which largely motivated it in the first place. It presented as it developed an alternative concept of a social and political order, one which had a strong appeal to a wide section of European society, not only to its fading elites.

In recent years there has been a great deal of research on the Counter-Revolution, more especially on its popular bases, which has helped in the process of understanding its origins and producing a more sympathetic approach, once confined largely to 'conservative' historians. The production of books covering aspects of the Counter-Revolution probably now approaches that of the more conventionally 'revolutionary' subjects. Much of this work is inaccessible to school sixth forms and, now that it is impossible to expect history undergraduates to have a reading knowledge of French, to university students as well. This book is intended to be a work of synthesis which will make some of this material more widely available. Although its framework is a narrative, it is also intended to indicate the main themes of the Counter-Revolution, its ideas, its practice, the conflicts and dilemmas within it, as well as its more lasting features. I have therefore made an attempt from time to time to stand back from the factual narrative in order to set the events in their wider context. That context included the rest of Europe, much of which at some time or other was occupied by the French. I have consequently departed briefly, at one point, from being concerned with France alone in order to look at the reaction to the Revolution elsewhere.

The book can make no pretension to be comprehensive either factually or in interpretation. That would require a much longer work, which might miss the readership at which it is aimed. Moreover, new material is appearing at such a pace that any judgement must be temporary. More detailed works are listed in the bibliography, although this has been confined to those available in English for the reason mentioned above. It is, therefore, necessarily very selective but provides enough guidance for readers who wish to pursue the subject further.

Because 'Counter-Revolution' was so widely and loosely defined, and even now is capable of many interpretations, I have been fairly selective. I have largely considered the Counter-Revolution in terms of the ideas and activities of the émigré princes and aristocracy, and of the popular insurrections which broke out from time to time within France. Many historians would now suggest that 'Anti-Revolution' is a better term for those rebellions, certainly in their earlier phases, but since the two strands were so interconnected I have stuck to the conventional usage.

The date at which to end a book is almost always a problem for historians and none more so than in the case of the Revolution and Counter-Revolution. They are both, as the expression is, 'permanent'. However, as in all things, a line must be drawn somewhere. 1830 makes more sense than, say, 1814 or 1799, because it was the point at which the original opponents of the Revolution made their last attempt from a position of power to check and reverse the revolutionary legacy and failed. The attempt was not abandoned: it was to be made by their successors but in increasingly forlorn circumstances.

Because this is a work of synthesis the debt is too vast to be individually acknowledged. It is to the historians on whose work I have drawn.

James Roberts

Maps

Map 1 The provinces of France in 1789
(Source: P.M. Jones, *The Peasantry in the French Revolution*)

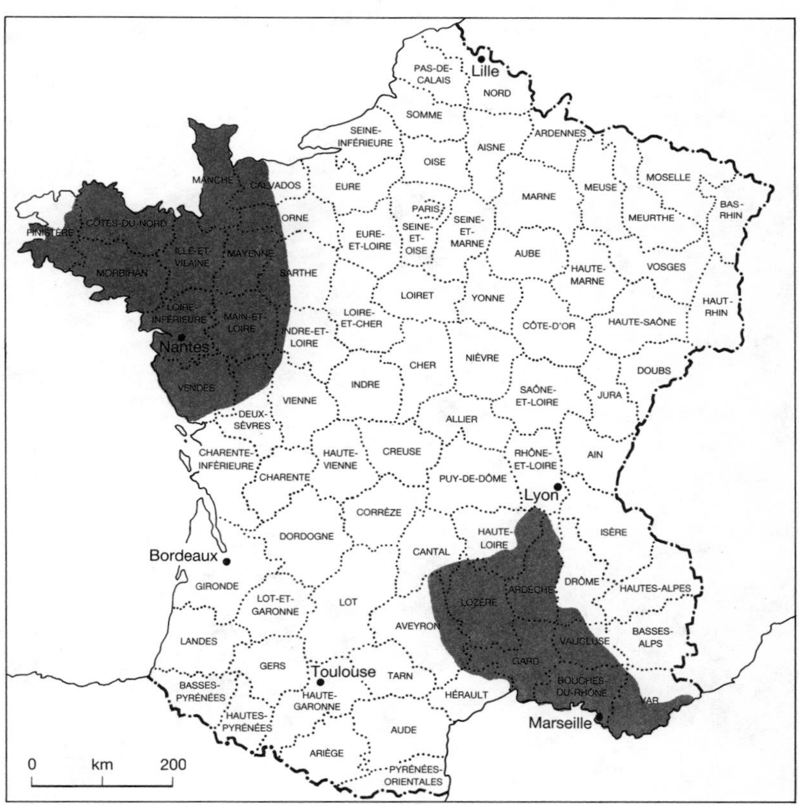

Map 2 Main areas of counter-revolutionary activity
(Source: P.M. Jones, *The Peasantry in the French Revolution*)

Introduction

The French Revolution never had the unified support of the whole French people. From its origins it stirred up formidable enemies, and each stage added yet another layer to the range of opponents. The conflict of Revolution and Counter-Revolution was to be one of the enduring legacies of the period, helping to shape French politics for another century or more, determining the attitudes of regions and classes, as well as historical interpretations. Distortion and misunderstanding were built into revolutionary conflict from the beginning. Who was, or was not, a friend of the Revolution lay very much in the eye of the beholder so that at some stage or other almost everybody could find themselves denounced as a counter-revolutionary agent. Such a charge came easily to Revolutionary governments, who tended to see their opponents, at least during the more intense phases of the Revolution, in fairly simple terms: the peasantry must have been led astray by aristocrats and priests; the émigrés were traitorous relics of a tyrannical past. That neat solution came naturally to politicians for whom the Revolution was a stage in the advance of humanity towards a more enlightened and just world and therefore anyone who resisted this was more than a traitor, he was also wicked. At a simpler level it also fitted into the thinking of a still credulous age, where conspirators lurked in the most unlikely places, and where disaster was always blamed on human misdeeds.

The opponents of the Revolution also had a similarly uncomplicated view of the conflict. Here was a struggle in defence of King and Church supported by a pious and still uncorrupted peasantry. The West particularly, the future heartland of Catholic royalism, lent itself to the creation of this type of myth, supported by numerous memoirs from the aristocracy and their connections. By the later nineteenth century, historians, although still taking a partisan view, were searching for a more sophisticated explanation of the motives behind Counter-

Revolution, especially the popular, peasant, aspect of it. That aspect came to be seen much more in terms of a movement with its own origins in discontents and traditions which had little to do with outside intervention. The émigré princes, similarly, although treated with less sympathy, can be seen as representing more than just a negative protest against their loss of place, a seventeenth-century Fronde inappropriately popping up more than a century later.

Revolutionary governments had every reason to take Counter-Revolution seriously even if they sometimes exaggerated its extent for motives of political advantage. Many of the policies of the revolutionary period make little sense unless they are seen as a response to the threats presented by opponents who challenged the fundamental principles on which those policies rested. For much of the revolutionary period large areas of France were effectively beyond the reach of government control. Administration had virtually collapsed in parts of the West as early as 1791 and full-scale war broke out there in 1793. It was not to be properly pacified until 1800. In the South serious disorders began even earlier, feeding on a long tradition of religious conflict. Even when attempts at open rebellion in the region were defeated it remained a centre of conspiracy and contact with the émigrés. Throughout much of the 1790s the association of brigandage and Counter-Revolution meant that large tracts of countryside were ungoverned, a haven for deserters and malcontents. In 1793 three of the major cities in the South – Marseilles, Lyons and Toulon – seemed to be on the brink of falling into the hands of Counter-Revolution. All of these revolts had links not just with the émigrés but also through them with foreign powers. From 1794 the British took these internal plots with increasing seriousness, even if not always consistently, and spent enormous sums of money in their support.

The émigrés alone would have been quite ineffectual, useful largely as a spectre to be paraded by politicians before the National Assembly for their own advantage. Their association with internal rebellion and foreign powers gave them more substance. So also did their ability to draw on an alternative body of ideas which may in some respects have looked back to a medieval concept of monarchy but in other respects was founded in the same doctrines of the Enlightenment as the Revolution itself, particularly the works of Montesquieu. Even if émigré politics owed more to personalities than to principle it could still call on some powerful traditions and sentiments. Many of those were to form part of Edmund Burke's eloquent and influential assault on the Revolution,

Reflections on the Revolution in France (1790). The emphasis placed by counter-revolutionary thought, as it developed over the next decade or so, on tradition, feeling, prejudice, the organic growth of societies, and religious faith was also running with the intellectual current of the time. Counter-Revolution offered a positive alternative to the revolutionary tradition. The politics of the emigration were not wholly an anachronism, neither were they static. The ultras who returned with Louis XVIII and the other princes in 1814 *had* learned something in spite of the well-known gibe. But it was not always the right or the most appropriate thing for the France of the 1820s and 1830s. The result was that the compromise represented by the Charter of 1814 appeared increasingly fragile and the threat from Counter-Revolution far from removed.

Counter-Revolution was to fail not just because of its ideology but because it was never the single great bloc in which revolutionaries in their more lurid moments affected to believe, or, for that matter, counter-revolutionaries also considered it. It was a loose assemblage of varying discontents and injuries of widely differing origins, each with its own solutions. Indeed, some were scarcely counter-revolutionary at all. Once revolutionary governments learned to distinguish these and acquired the men, materials and techniques to deal with them, Counter-Revolution could be crushed. Even within the ideology of Counter-Revolution, properly understood, however, there were massive and irreconcilable contradictions, and especially insoluble dilemmas over attitudes towards the popular movements which could be obscured for a while but, once restored to power, reinforced the other failings of Bourbon royalism and helped bring about its defeat in 1830. It was not a defeat which was regarded as final. In its various forms opposition to the Revolution survived into the twentieth century until its definitive end in 1944.

1

The Politics of the Emigration

On 17 July 1789 a few small groups of Court nobility left France and went into exile. The most prominent figure among them was the king's youngest brother, the comte d'Artois. The others included the prince de Condé and his son the duc de Bourbon, and Artois' sons the ducs de Berry and d'Angoulême. They left in part because their schemes and policies had collapsed with the fall of the Bastille and the subsequent recall of Necker, but also because a temporary withdrawal for their own safety was thought advisable. It was a fairly light-hearted, even fashionable, departure to allow the political temperature to cool. 'We'll be back in three months', Artois told Esterhazy at the frontier. 'We expected to spend three months at Tournay and then to return to find everything as it was', remembered the marquise de Falaizeau. In fact, most of those who left at this time were not to return, if at all, for the next twenty-five years.

They were by no means the whole of the emigration or even a representative portion of it, socially or ideologically. The emigration was to include many strands, some of which co-operated uneasily, while there was mutual loathing among the others. Only a minority of the nobility ever emigrated, most managing either to live out the Revolution in obscurity, or in many other cases taking advantage of the opportunities it offered: a high proportion, for example, of Napoleonic officials and generals were drawn from the old nobility, most of whom had furthered their careers during the Revolution itself. By far the greater proportion of the émigrés in the revolutionary period were from the Third Estate or the clergy; many fell in the category of what would now be called refugees, such as the peasants displaced by the advancing and retreating armies.

The numbers have been variously estimated but can possibly be put at 150,000. By the standards of the twentieth century it is modest indeed. Many émigrés came and went several times over; others on the lists never went at all, like Mme de la Tour du Pin's mother who spent the whole of the Revolution in a French convent yet had her name on a list and her property confiscated. Mme du Pin herself was on no list even though she was out of France for almost the whole period between 1794 and 1800. Only a minority of émigrés, perhaps about 5000, ever fought actively against the Revolution, and that very briefly, while most led lives of obscurity, even poverty, finding their way back to France as the opportunity presented itself. The emigration meant, in Vidalenc's phrase, 'the sum of private adventures'. The range of experience in exile was enormous, as was the geographical spread of the emigration. About 10,000 found their way to America, including Mme du Pin, who claimed to have found simple pleasures as a dairy farmer among 'her good friends the savages'.

Yet the term émigré had already acquired the meaning it was to retain in revolutionary demonology whether in this period or even down to the present day: that of a small group of backward-looking, frivolous individuals attempting to restore an outworn social and political system in their own selfish interests but ultimately condemned to defeat and nullity. The 'Court' emigration around Artois fitted part at least of this description. Artois established himself first at Turin, his father-in-law's capital, and then, during the spring of 1791, at Coblenz in the Rhineland. There were other centres, such as that which developed around Condé at Worms. Although Artois and his Court were only to be at Coblenz for about a year it became a synonym for a certain style of conduct, a whole attitude of mind. In both places it tried the patience of its hosts with its outrageous behaviour (even while claiming to boost the native economy with its spending power). When they eventually left Coblenz ninety silver dinner plates, amongst other things, disappeared with them. It cost the Elector 60,000 livres to replace his linen. The émigré Court's obsession with the petty detail of precedence and ceremonial, its extravagance, its intrigue, and its recreation of all the worst aspects of Versailles horrified the provincial nobility who found their way there. 'Extravagance, gambling, debauchery, intriguing, personal interest, ambition, pride, stupidity, selfishness, bad faith dominated there with as much force as in any other European Court', said de Maleissye, a former officer in the *gardes françaises*. D'Espinchal found at Coblenz what he described as 'the style, the attitudes, the intrigues of which the princes had more than ever reason to purge their circles. Little groups of women and hangers-on, card parties whose enormous stakes insulted the poor and respectable nobility who watched them.' 'A sewer of the intrigues, cabals, stupidities, fawnings and silliness of the old Court', wrote another nobleman. There was an air of unreality which led Marshal de Castries to call it 'this Court in Utopia'. Some, like Cazalès who was a long way from being a moderate, were unable to bear it and went home.

Yet even while they shared in the almost universal scorn, revolutionary governments appeared to take the émigrés very seriously indeed, as the large number of measures directed at them indicates. Why this was so when at the same time the princes' emigration became a byword for ineffective frivolity needs some explanation. Partly it was a response to the pressures of revolutionary politics, where various groups found the émigrés a useful stick with which to beat the government. Also, of course, the presence on the borders of the king's relatives and connections, all intriguing with foreign powers against the Revolution and with disaffected regions at home, and at the same time attempting to form their own armies, was bound to create unease in a still insecure regime which had a tendency to blame every misfortune on a conspiracy engineered from abroad in alliance with their unenlightened friends at home.

But to focus purely on the negative aspects of the emigration is to miss much of its point. The princes' emigration, like other branches of the Counter-Revolution, was rarely an effort to restore the *ancien régime* in its entirety, unchanged in any detail. Indeed, there were very few even amongst the so-called 'pures', those who claimed their principles were untarnished by compromise, who believed that no change was needed. Most of the aristocratic émigrés had joined in the political assault on the *ancien régime* with enthusiasm. The often-repeated jest of one émigré that the best thing about the *ancien régime* was its abuses was not meant to be taken seriously. The dividing point in the emigration, as in the Revolution, was the shape of that reform. For the most part, counter-revolutionary opinion amongst the émigrés drew on a body of thought rooted as much in the Enlightenment and a view of French history as the Revolution, even if with a different perspective and vastly different conclusions. It is in this sense, as Goodwin long ago pointed out, that the origins of Counter-Revolution precede the Revolution itself although they could only be focused once revolution had broken out. They are to be found not just in rival personalities and ambitions, important though they are, but in an attitude to the nature of royal government and its relationship to traditional institutions, privileges and customs. The personal squabbles of the old Court factions which the émigrés took with them into exile, the sheer silliness of much of their behaviour, can divert attention from this and obscure the fact that the princes and their allies represented something more than just the aimless plotting of a defunct and unemployed social group. If that is all they had been they would scarcely have been able to call on the support, even devotion, of a diverse number of individuals many of whom were perfectly sensible and honourable people. Indeed, many of the elements of counter-revolutionary thought survived through much of the nineteenth century long after their apparently definitive defeat in 1830. That was not just because of romantic attachment to a lost cause but because the ideas were founded in a long tradition which still seemed to have relevance to the problems of France. In short, they were part of a long-running debate on the nature of French government and society which was brought to a head and whose battle-lines were defined in the crisis of 1787–9.

One of the commonest charges against late eighteenth-century royal government was that of 'ministerial despotism' by which was meant that the Crown was being influenced by its ministers to ride roughshod over established rights and privileges in its drive to create a more centralised, bureaucratic, monarchy. There was enough substance in this to give it credence; royal governments were reforming ones, even if fitful and ultimately ineffective. However, when a united government chose a course of action and could rely on the support of the Crown it was clear that customary rights and institutions were powerless to stop it. The brief episode in 1771 when Maupeou reconstructed the *parlements* was evidence of this. Only the accession of a new king produced a change of heart. The *parlements* saw themselves as the principal defenders of customary and provincial rights against the potential despotism of unchecked central government. The type of minister increasingly to be found in central government and at the level of *Intendant* only reinforced these fears. They were often men of recent nobility, trained in the royal bureaucracy, talented and ambitious, ready instruments of a centralising policy. Calonne was just such an example: a former *Intendant* whose charm, ability, ambition and cultivation of the right social circles brought him in 1783 to the post of Controller General of the Finances. Another was Vergennes, whose death in February 1787 on the eve of the First Assembly of the Notables was to help create the confusion in government which paved the way for the defeat of the reform proposals.

These anxieties could bring together strands of opposition to royal government which were in other respects widely different. In the case of the princes and the Court aristocracy, however, they were to be entangled in the personal rivalries of *ancien régime* government which were to provide rich sources of intrigue in the early years of the emigration. By its very nature *ancien régime* government proceeded by intrigue in the absence of any formalised means of expressing alternative policies such as a regularly convened Assembly. The main object of the Princes of the Blood was to secure that place on the Council from which they had been excluded in the seventeenth century. In this they met the resolute opposition of not just the king but also of Marie-Antoinette who led the most important Court faction. The queen's marriage to the future Louis XVI in 1770 had been the dynastic seal on the reversal of traditional French foreign policy which in 1756 had brought it into alliance with Austria. As such she was regarded with deep dislike by everybody who saw that alliance as the origin of the disasters to French arms which had followed. The queen's faction consisted of the connections of those ministers who had supported the Austrian alliance, such as the baron de Breteuil, from 1783 the *ministre de la Maison du Roi* (roughly the equivalent of a modern Minister of the Interior). Calonne, on the other hand, became attached to the rival group. The Austrian issue lay at the heart of the divisions at Court but they were infinitely complex because of clashes of personality probably made worse by the queen's tendency to see most things in highly personalised terms. The labyrinthine quarrels of the Court went into emigration along with the people involved. Thus, the Breteuil and Calonne dispute was carried on with ferocious intensity even though many of their points of political difference may have been slender. What mattered was the conflict of ambition and deep mutual antipathy.

In 1787 when Calonne presented his reform proposals to the Assembly of Notables he had a formidable range of enemies, with the queen at the head, set against him. Nevertheless, there was little unity among these opponents and no clear set of alternatives other than changes in detail. The Court nobility was itself divided, with Artois and Condé supporting Calonne; there was little sympathy between Court nobility and provincial aristocracy; and the *parlements* were normally incapable of resisting a determined government. Calonne was dismissed because he was isolated and, above all, had lost the support of the king, not because of any unified opposition based on agreed principle. Indeed, his successor Brienne was to follow a broadly similar policy. It was the events themselves which brought together some of these inchoate and normally contradictory elements and provided the working basis of the princely and aristocratic Counter-Revolution although the tensions and contradictions were never far below the surface, while the factional rancour was to survive into the emigration. The first of those events was the reaction of the Paris *Parlement* to the imminent reconstruction of the judicial system by Lamoignon's May Edicts in 1788. Uneasily edged into the role of leaders of a popular protest movement, the *Parlement* nevertheless felt obliged to resist such a drastic reduction in their powers. By the end of the year they were largely to have faded from the scene but the Fundamental Laws of the Kingdom, issued by the Paris *Parlement* on 3 May, were to remain part of the programme of the section of the Counter-Revolution which represented the provincial aristocracy, elaborated in the course of 1788, securing the support of the princes and triumphing in the Royal Session of 23 June 1789 when apparently the three strands of Crown, princes and provinces sealed their agreement.

The Fundamental Laws contained nothing very new. They were virtually a summary of the claims made from time to time in the course of the century by *parlements* during their clashes with the Crown. The main points were regular meetings of the Estates General to consent to taxation, respect for provincial customs, and prompt trial.

The Memorandum of the Princes of the Blood in December 1788 supported the demand of the Paris *Parlement* for the Estates General to be called in its traditional (i.e. 1614) form and stressed the value of the rights of the Orders as a barrier against despotism. Significantly, the princes also presented themselves as members of the nobility and defenders of its rights ('their main title is that of gentlemen'). They were in effect moving towards an alliance with the provincial aristocracy.

It was a link made even more clearly in the Declaration of 23 June issued by the king at a Royal Session. Although its main purpose was to impose a programme of reform on a recalcitrant Third Estate and set the limits to further concession it became a central document of the Counter-Revolution, a sort of treaty of alliance between three varied elements, the princes, the Crown and the provincial aristocracy. Much of it was meant to be acceptable to the Third Estate but even more to the aristocracy: regular meetings of the Estates General, provincial Estates (albeit with double representation for the Third and meetings in common), the end of *lettres de cachet*, a reduction in the powers of the *Intendant*, and above all the retention of a society based on a framework of Orders. The power of the Crown would be preserved but it would also be balanced by the recognition of the rights of the Orders. Through the years of emigration it was a document that the princes were extremely reluctant to modify. If anything they took an even harder line, at least in the first years of the emigration. It gave a coherence to the disparate forces of the Counter-Revolution. Only slowly was the future Louis XVIII in emigration to be prised away from its principles and even though much of it was gone by 1800 there were still echoes in 1814.

Yet the contradictions were never far below the surface. The émigré princes, who included the comte de Provence from June 1791, were in almost constant conflict with the king and queen, especially the latter, whose dislike for Artois and Calonne could be venomous. However, there was little clash on principle other than the claim by the princes to be represented on the Council. They wanted to share in that power from which they felt they had been unreasonably excluded. Yet they did not want to see the monarchy weakened because that would diminish the very influence they sought. Their complaint against Louis XVI was that he had allowed the Crown, a family affair of which he was the temporary head, to be 'captured' by the Revolution. He had failed in his first responsibility, which was to hand it on to his successors untarnished. The point was made bluntly, even brutally, to the king by Provence in a letter on 10 September 1791; 'As the present holder of the throne you have inherited from your ancestors, you can neither alienate its ancient rights nor destroy the constitutional base on which it is founded.' The emphasis on an old constitution and the description of the Crown as the protector of the rights of the Orders, were in line with the Declaration of 23 June. The letter itself was the first of a series of similar reaffirmations issued at appropriate moments by the exiled princes. In the end, however, whatever concessions were made to the aristocracy, real authority remained with the royal family, an authority which Louis XVI, in the opinion of the princes, had sacrificed.

The provincial aristocracy who found their way to Coblenz or who stayed in France to weave their conspiracies saw the balance of power somewhat differently. From their point of view the Crown was powerful enough and needed to be checked by that combination of customary rights and institutions which had been eroded by a centralising monarchy and destroyed by the Revolution. The extravagant antics of the Court at Coblenz only confirmed all the distaste they had always felt for the parasites of Versailles who had drained the resources of France at the expense of the honest provincial nobleman. Relationships between the princes and the aristocracy of this type were frequently marked by incomprehension and contempt. The Revolution did not necessarily heal the gap: the religious issues, for example, which moved the populations, and their local aristocracy, in some regions were barely understood by a sceptic like Artois (until his conversion after 1804). Some of the later problems of the Restoration were to be rooted in these misunderstandings.

Many of the characteristics and prejudices of the provincial nobleman can be found embodied in the comte d'Antraigues. He is worth looking at in a little detail because he also played a central part in the policy-making of the emigration through his role as spymaster and purveyor of information to the princes and whoever else he could find to buy it. He was deeply attached to his native province, the Vivarais, whose rights and privileges he wished to see restored, and for that reason was a defender of the *parlements* among whose members at Toulouse and in Paris he had many close friends. It was in defence of the *parlements* that he wrote his best-selling *Memoir on the Estates General* in 1788.

Although this was written as a piece of special pleading at a time of political crisis it nevertheless illustrates the point that the aristocratic Counter-Revolution rested on more than mere self-interest. It was a work well within the framework of the Enlightenment, owing much to Montesquieu whose *Spirit of the Laws* (1748) constituted the century's main philosophic defence of the limitation of power through a balance of interests and traditional institutions. The existence of an old constitution, the moral dimension of the state, the duty of government to respect individual liberty and the customs of various groups could all help to make Montesquieu a quarry for liberalism or for some of the principles of aristocratic Counter-Revolution just as he was for the Revolution itself. It is a reminder of a point we shall come across again, that Revolution and Counter-Revolution could draw on the same philosophic stock but take it to different conclusions.

The influence of this on d'Antraigues demonstrates that he was no bucolic squireen but rather a cultivated, sceptical, tolerant (except in politics) product of his times, moving easily in intellectual and Court circles even though his contempt for the latter was profound. Power, he thought, should be checked by a hierarchy of institutions and privileges such as the *parlements*, with a regular meeting of the Estates General as the representative body of the kingdom consulting with the Crown. The Third Estate's representation could be doubled as long as the society of Orders was retained. His own dependence largely on seigneurial dues reinforced his defence of them – the August 4th decrees, with their abolition of many dues, were largely to ruin him. Background, intellectual conviction, and personal need were also supported by a formidable list of prejudices which he pursued with unrelenting malice and vindictiveness. He had a low opinion of the political sense of the Court aristocracy and the princes; a strong antipathy towards the queen; a passionate hatred of Breteuil. He made no distinction between all these or anyone else who was perceived as slacking in opposition to his ideal of a monarchy limited through custom and Order rather than wealth. In that respect he was typical of the aristocratic emigration.

Although Artois had no clear idea of what policy to pursue when he left France, a strategy was steadily evolved by the princes which was to remain unchanged in its essentials throughout the emigration. It consisted of a two-pronged armed attack on the Revolution from outside and inside France. There was to be just one tentative and half-hearted departure from this under British pressure in 1796–7 when an attempt to secure a restoration by constitutional means came close to succeeding. The first object was to secure the support of the European powers for armed intervention in France, with the émigré armies playing a leading role. As the second element of the attack the princes attempted to encourage risings inside France. Success in the first part of this strategy depended on convincing the European powers that their struggle was the common cause of monarchical Europe and that the king was no longer a free agent. Therefore the comte d'Artois was the man to deal with as the true representative of the interests of the Crown. The personalities and conduct of the princes and their circle were, however, seldom such as to inspire confidence: the Court of Turin was glad to see them go in 1791; their behaviour hardly improved at Coblenz. 'They think only of their romantic ideas, their vengeance, their personal interests', said the Emperor Leopold in the same year. Even apart from such considerations, none of the European powers, with the eccentric exception of Sweden, saw its interests involved in war with France – indeed the very opposite, since France's difficulties allowed them to pursue their ambitions unhindered. Those ambitions lay in the East, especially in Poland, where Austria, Prussia and Russia kept a close watch on each other. Even apart from this, it was difficult to take the appeals of Artois seriously when the king showed no desire to be 'rescued'. 'It is up to the king of France to show he is worth supporting', said the Spanish first minister. 'It would be pointless as well as impossible to make him king in spite of himself.' That was almost exactly Artois' policy: 'to save the king in spite of himself'. This was justified by the argument that the king was a prisoner. Therefore, as Condé argued early in 1790, the king's actions, because they were constrained, were null and patriotic loyalty to the best interests of the monarchy demanded that the émigrés should not falter but rather 'redouble' their efforts.

The long continuity of the princes' policy gives it almost an inevitability, as if there were no alternative. There was, of course. Even within the circle of the princes others urged a different policy. One of Artois' closest friends, the comte de Vaudreuil, who had accompanied him into exile on 17 July, argued for patience and caution, the slow task of working on a change of opinion in France. The Revolution, he understood, was the expression of the national will which could only be overcome by an equivalent force of opinion: 'Opinion started the Revolution, opinion will put the Counter-Revolution to work.' The makings of that reversal were present in the provinces in the deep sense of deception, so he believed, felt at the measures taken by the Assembly. It needed to be worked on by 'wisdom and persuasion rather than by force and severity'. It was therefore essential, he argued, to avoid calling in foreign powers which could only place the royal family in danger, put France at the mercy of its international enemies and rivals, and put the princes in the position of traitors. 'Foreign troops would terrify the kingdom instead of rallying it to the right cause; and all good Frenchmen would feel a well-founded revulsion against rallying to foreigners.' There must be agreement between the Court and the emigration; and, echoing the words of the Spanish minister, 'to serve them in spite of themselves is impossible'. In short, a policy of caution, unity of method and aim, avoiding embroiling the powers in France's internal affairs, and relying on France itself, above all the provinces ('it is from them alone that the monarchy can expect its salvation'), to save the nation, was what Vaudreuil urged on Artois His advice, delivered in the course of 1789–90, was not just sensible but, in the end, right. In almost every particular his warnings as to the consequences of relying on foreign armed intervention, that it would place the princes in the position of traitors and rally even the hesitant French behind the Revolution, turned out to be true. Unfortunately it was advice which was never taken, partly because he was himself incapable of sustaining it. In a sense this was due to his skills as a courtier (and taste – he loved Coblenz as he had loved Versailles) which made it difficult for him to be disagreeable to whatever circle he found himself in. Away from Artois he could write his advice. In his company he gave way. The result was that Artois followed his instincts, which were almost invariably incorrect right to the end of his life, and the worst possible course in the initial stages of the emigration was adopted. Once war had broken out in 1792, and been extended in 1793, the lines of policy suggested by Vaudreuil no longer had any relevance and Vaudreuil himself had long abandoned them.

It must, of course, in justice to Artois, be remembered that he and the other princes were subject to the pressures of their circle and the increasing numbers of aristocratic officers and provincial gentry who went into emigration. They may have left in order to escape the increasing harassment of the revolutionary authorities; but it was also in the expectation that they would shortly be returning with one of the émigré armies and in alliance with foreign powers. Such feelings were especially strong after the failure of the king's escape attempt from Paris in June 1791. Now more than ever he could be regarded as a prisoner. True kingship therefore lay outside the borders in the person of Artois (rather than Provence) and the ideal was that of Henri IV who in the late sixteenth century had reconquered his kingdom from rebellious factions. The provincial émigrés often kept in touch with their native regions with this future return in mind. De Maleyssie, whose contemptuous remarks on Coblenz were quoted earlier, nevertheless returned to France to gather information on its behalf even though he was aware how little it understood the problems involved. D'Espinchal too might have been disparaging about Coblenz but also saw in Artois more 'kingly' possibilities. In short, the émigrés gathered in the Rhineland were not the type to wait on events. Temperament and conviction, not to say financial necessity, forced an active policy on them and on the princes.

The policy of Turin and Coblenz was also rejected by the Court and not just on the grounds of the unreliable personalities of the princes. The king's reluctance to be rescued was not due to his normal infirmity of purpose. Indeed, in many respects this aspect of Louis XVI's character has been overstated. He had a clear idea of the interests of the Crown and unlike the princes had to defend them on a daily basis. The Court's policy was very consistent at least down to the beginning of 1792 when the international situation changed. What he, and the queen, feared, was that a foreign invasion, led by the princes and their army, would impose on him a settlement in which he would be the 'prisoner' of the aristocracy. 'If the émigrés were to succeed', said the queen, 'they will be making the law for a long time to come; it will be impossible to refuse them anything; it is to undertake too great an obligation to owe the crown to them.' 'The émigrés re-entering France in arms, everything is lost', she wrote to Leopold in October 1791; 'there would be a slavery worse than the preceding one.' Louis had to prevent Artois acting as if the king was no longer a free agent, just as, later on, in 1791, he had to resist Provence's efforts to get the European powers to recognise him as Regent. In February 1791 Artois, through his representative at the Diet of Ratisbon, once again made the claim that the king was not free when he called for support 'in view of the captivity of my brother and older relatives' (who at that stage included Provence). The king's attitude was quite clear: to show that he was a free agent by remaining in France and blocking the princes' efforts at forming a coalition to invade the country. Instead, the king aimed to create an 'Armed Congress' of the powers to put pressure on France for constitutional change in a direction favourable to the Court.

The king's capacity to act swiftly to protect his interests against the schemes of the princes was shown when, in November 1790, he appointed Breteuil as his representative just two weeks after the arrival of Calonne in Turin to advise Artois. Calonne brought with him the weight of his administrative and political experience and he was to be, until 1792, virtually the first minister of the emigration. At heart he was still the bureaucratic centralist he had always been but he was able to adjust these views to the princes' programme in the interests of his ambition to return to power. Such a prospect could only fill the queen with horror and the appointment of Breteuil, a personal enemy of Calonne, was a calculated snub both to him and to Artois. In fact, the views of Breteuil and Calonne on the nature of the monarchy were probably much the same but their long record of mutual animosity made any compromise out of the question. Breteuil may have been more supple and realistic in his approach to the Revolution, willing to reach some accommodation with its leaders on certain principles in the interests of retaining the reality of power for the Crown. Nevertheless he was a long way from thinking in terms of a limited monarchy of the type favoured either by aristocrats like d'Antraigues or constitutional monarchists like Malouet and Mounier. His policy of working with the revolutionaries in order to deflect them into more acceptable directions was deeply suspect to the emigration, while to Calonne, who understood his policy only too well, he was simply a rival for eventual power. In either case here was a new figure of hate for the émigrés to add to the already ample list.

Breteuil's instructions were quite straightforward: to block the policy of the princes to secure a foreign invasion with themselves at its head. Such a policy would end in the king becoming the 'prisoner' of the aristocracy. The king and queen made personal appeals to the European monarchs with whom Artois was trying to make contact to restrain the princes and not to receive them. The reluctance of the Emperor to do so illustrates the success of the policy. 'Our whole policy must come down to diverting the ideas of invasion which the émigrés might attempt on their own', the king wrote in January 1791 to Breteuil. 'It would be France's undoing if the émigrés were in the front line and if they merely had the help of a few Powers.' There was a farcical aspect to all this, with many European capitals having three representatives of France: the official ambassador of the government, an agent of the princes, and one of Breteuil's men. Nevertheless for the time being the Court's policy worked since the powers could scarcely take seriously the claims of the princes to be acting on behalf of a captive king whose agents were assuring them differently. The princes, and Calonne, ever optimistic, were reduced to clutching at any hint of a change of heart by Leopold who in fact instructed his representatives to do nothing for them.

Just such a change of heart seemed to appear in the summer of 1791 as a result of the failure of the Court's 'flight to Varennes'. The princes had been pressing the king to flee from the beginning although the actual flight took them by surprise. Its failure may not, however, have been altogether unwelcome to them. Leopold felt obliged to respond in some way to the humiliations heaped on his sister. The Padua Circular, in July, an appeal from him to the European powers for joint action in defence of the French royal family, and the Declaration of Pillnitz a month later, a joint declaration from Austria and Prussia of their intention to restore firm monarchical government in France, raised émigré hopes. In fact, even if Pillnitz did say that it was in response to the princes' appeals, and in consultation with them, they had no part in its drafting, it fell far short of their wishes, and was so hedged about with conditions as to be virtually worthless. Austrian policy was to intimidate the radicals inside France so that the royal family was safe from their threats but otherwise to leave the French to flounder in their domestic difficulties. That seemed to have been achieved when, in September, the king accepted the constitution. The appeal by Artois and Provence in the letter to the king of 10 September, urging him to reject the constitution and attaching the Declaration of Pillnitz in support, had failed.

The émigré princes were now apparently in a dead-end. The king's appeals to them to return were rejected. They restated their view that the National Assembly had usurped the function of the only legitimate assembly, the Estates General, whose authority had rested on the *cahiers*. The king was bound to pass on the kingdom in the form in which he had received it. Artois again asserted, in November, his belief that the king was not a free agent. All this seemed to the Court obstructive, negative and unrealistic. 'Cain, Cain!' the queen is reported to have said after Provence's sarcastic reply to the Assembly's order that he should return. What the princes stood for nevertheless represented a programme with deep roots in French tradition and custom, and a strong attraction in provincial France which stretched beyond the narrow confines of the 'privileged' Orders. The loyalties which it commanded were to be enduring ones which survived repeated disappointments as well as the incompetence of its leaders. In the winter of 1791–2, however, there appeared to be little hope of success. The low point was the dispersal of the émigré armies on their territories by the Electors of Mainz and Trier in response to a decree of the National Assembly. The émigrés faced a winter of considerable hardship.

In fact events were starting to move in a more hopeful direction for them, that is towards war. This had nothing to do with their efforts but more with developments in France itself and Austria's diplomatic relations. The war against Turkey came to an end in August 1791 and so freed Austria from commitments on the eastern frontier. In France political groups on both wings began to see advantages in an aggressive foreign policy: the Brissotins thought they could achieve power by a popular anti-Austrian position; and other groupings, particularly around Lafayette, also thought that war would bring them to power. The moderates were steadily outflanked by this combination of interests pursuing a similar policy for different ends. Individuals such as Robespierre on the extreme left who saw sinister forces behind the rising demands for war were also isolated. The Court still held to its policy of securing an 'Armed Congress' which would stop short of invasion. But an alternative was being formulated, outlined by Breteuil in December to the Emperor: that in a disastrous war the French would turn to the king to save them from the consequences of defeat and internal chaos. In the early spring of 1792, however, the Court counted for little as the moderate Feuillant ministry was replaced by a Brissotin one and, in Austria, the less cautious Francis succeeded Leopold. On 20 April the French declared war on Austria, which was joined by the Empire and Prussia with whom a formal alliance had been signed in February.

In all this the émigrés had been marginal except in so far as their presence in the Rhineland had provided an irritant in diplomatic relations and their optimistic estimates of the unpreparedness of the French armies had supported similar assessments of the military situation by the Austrians and Prussians. It was an optimism which remained when war was declared: 'it will be a walk-over', announced an émigré nobleman. However, the émigrés were to remain on the sidelines in spite of their hopes that they would play a leading role in the invasion which would sweep them to power. Neither Austria nor Prussia had the slightest intention of allowing anything other than a subsidiary position to the ill-equipped, ill-disciplined and over-officered émigré armies. Relations between the allies and the émigrés were to be bad from start to finish. The émigrés had one last opportunity to wreck the policies of the king and queen. Now that war had come it was the Court's object to carry out their aim of seeing that a swift victory by the allies would be followed by the restoration of a secure monarchy, Church and property but in an atmosphere of reconciliation (except for 'extremists') and free of foreign interference. The manifesto that the king wanted issued on these lines was in the end drawn up by an émigré and bore the imprint of their vengeful intentions. The Brunswick Manifesto had the opposite effect of what was intended, hardening attitudes within the revolutionary camp.

Louis XVI and Breteuil were still able to resist the pressures from the princes in one respect. Artois, and Provence when he emigrated, had both hoped that a regency could be declared and so enable them to exercise power in an official capacity. This was all the more important now that an invasion was imminent. By the time the king received the request he was in reality a prisoner after the second revolution on 10 August. Nevertheless, the reply sent in early September agreed to a regency as long as Calonne was dismissed. There was no hesitation.

Calonne departed for Naples. The regency, however, did not follow because Breteuil had managed to make it contingent on Austrian approval and that was not forthcoming.

All this intrigue was soon to be entirely academic except to add further weight to the émigré belief in the incorrigible duplicity of Austria and Breteuil. On 20 September the Prussians gave way before the superior numbers and artillery of the French at Valmy. The retreat through eastern France was a horror story of rain, mud, plunder by Prussians and peasants alike. The émigré army fell apart. Only Condé's army, which had not been involved, remained in existence under Austrian control. Artois and Provence, briefly arrested at Aachen for debt, began ten years or so of wandering over much of Europe before ultimately settling down in England.

The defeat at Valmy ended one phase of the emigration, apparently in disaster, a disaster greater for the nobility than for Prussia since it ended their hopes of a triumphant return and the restoration of their position. Yet the main lines of counter-revolutionary policy had been formed and from these the émigrés, those that is who resisted the temptation to return, were not to waver until the Restoration. The ideology rested on the 'alliance' implicit in the various pronouncements of 1788–9, culminating in the Royal Session of 23 June. Broadly that involved the restoration of a monarchy limited by the association in government of the Princes of the Blood, a regularly convened Estates General, separated by Orders, and strong local government based on the old provinces under the leadership of their aristocracies. This was to be achieved by external invasion and internal subversion. By the end of 1792 both of these wings of counter-revolutionary activity had received a severe check but nevertheless the pattern was established.

However, it is not too difficult to spot the flaws in all this. The alliance of princes and aristocracy was subject to strains from beginning to end, both social and political. The invasion of 1792 had helped obscure them, and the enthusiasm, felt for example by Chateaubriand, at the apparent reforging of the ancient unity of princes and aristocracy in the advancing army softened resentments felt at the contrast in conditions. Defeat crushed that illusion. The necessary modifications, as time passed, to the émigré programme to bring it into line with changing reality increased those strains. In the end the contradictions which lay at the root of them were to be a reason for the final failure of the Bourbons. At least the outbreak of war apparently solved the problem of foreign help but the Counter-Revolution of the 'exterior' was always to be a prisoner of its allies. No European power went to war purely for ideological reasons, even if some individual ministers might have seen things like that. All the nations which found themselves at war with France, and that included most at some time or other, felt that their national interests were at stake and could only be defended by a war. If that war ceased to be winnable or the cost was too high then they sought peace regardless of the Counter-Revolution. For Austria and Prussia, anyway, events inside France were frequently of secondary importance to their eastern frontiers. The entry of Britain into the war in February 1793 provided a fresh ally but British aims were no more those of the émigrés than Austria's or Prussia's had been. Other sources of pressure on the allies were needed in order to keep their support.

One means of securing this was to show that the Counter-Revolution of the 'interior' was not only spreading but that it looked to the émigrés for inspiration and leadership. The arrival in Turin and, later, Coblenz of emissaries from the provinces with optimistic accounts of budding revolt and seeking princely approval gave substance to this policy. This was the second 'prong' of the émigré attack on the Revolution, to exploit the discontent within France at the failings of the Revolution. It was, of course, the advice offered by Vaudreuil among others. Yet from the beginning, Artois, the other princes and many of the aristocracy were to get it wrong. That was partly because of political ineptitude and partly because of the unreality of the world of the emigration; but it was also because of a fundamental misunderstanding as to the nature of the popular Counter-Revolution. It rarely coincided with the political aims of the princes and their émigré allies. Even in the case of the provincial nobility there was frequently a basic divergence of aim. An ambitious plan for a rising in Brittany put together in 1791 by the marquis de la Rouerie developed a broad popular base but its objective was the reassertion of the provincial liberties destroyed by the Revolution. Like the popular revolts it was essentially local in its origins and purposes compared to the national scale on which the princes based their schemes.

It was a misunderstanding which easily developed into mistrust, making an alliance between the two elements difficult to achieve not just during the revolutionary period itself but into the Restoration and beyond. It also made it the more difficult to convince the British that the popular insurrections which began to unfold with increasing seriousness from 1790 had as their aim the restoration of the former system. It is to these movements that we must now turn.

2

The Popular Counter-Revolution

The encouragement of rebellions within France was not only essential if the allies were to take the émigrés seriously, as well as being a condition of any British support, it also made military and political sense. In the end it was the policy which was to succeed, although in considerably changed circumstances. The émigrés were anyway convinced that the French people had been led astray in their search for novelties by a handful of wicked men. Once these were suitably punished then a volatile nation would return gratefully to the traditional order for which they really hankered. This illusion was not to be dented even by the hostile reception given to the émigrés by the peasantry during the brief invasion of 1792. It was not, however, just their usual infinite capacity for self-delusion which was responsible for this. The princes for the most part were deeply ignorant of provincial France. They had to rely for information on spy networks such as the Paris Agency which passed on its observations to d'Antraigues. Not only was it often pure fiction to start with, it was selected by d'Antraigues to reinforce his own opinions. In addition, the princes received information from various disaffected individuals who found their way to their Court from rebellious areas. They always had a particular case to present and always gave a highly optimistic view of their chances of success. Wishful thinking ran deep in counter-revolutionary circles.

If information was frequently inaccurate and out-of-date, it was made worse by the lack of understanding of the motivation and objectives of the disturbances and risings in southern and western France, the two areas most deeply affected by discontent with the Revolution. It was a Counter-Revolution quite different in origins and composition from anything known to the emigration, mystifying even, in its passions and intensity, eccentric in its military tactics, brutal and barbarous in its methods. Not surprisingly, some émigrés, steeped in the conventions of eighteenth-century warfare, quite apart from eighteenth-century scepticism, who arrived to join the peasant rebels were contemptuous of what they found, a contempt that was reciprocated by those on the spot.

Here were genuinely popular movements, autonomous in their origins, aims and leadership, neither manipulated, in spite of the suspicions and charges of revolutionary governments, by aristocrats and priests, nor ever under the control of the émigré princes and their allies. Because of this many historians now prefer to call these movements an Anti-Revolution rather than Counter-Revolution; that is, they were directed *against* the Revolution and its demands rather than *for* the restoration of the structure of the *ancien régime*, although they were royalist in the sense of supporting the monarchy. However, in the short term, they made the threat of Counter-Revolution more of a reality than the émigrés alone ever could, presented the Revolution with some of the most serious threats to its existence and at times forced on its governments important changes of direction, while in the long term, especially in the case of the West, they produced lasting changes in the map of French political attitudes.

Discontent with, or indifference towards, the Revolution was common enough at various times in most parts of France during the revolutionary period. The Revolution made a great many demands on the French people. In pursuit of those demands the revolutionary state stretched its tentacles into areas which the *ancien régime* had left alone. The officials of the more aggressive central government were also representatives of the urban legal class most resented by the peasantry, and moreover the class which had gained most from the Revolution. For most other people the Revolution was a disaster and not surprisingly at various times most parts of France are to be found in some form of resistance to it. It was only within the South and West that this was strong enough to produce armed rebellion against the authorities sufficient at times to appear to threaten the Revolution and offer the prospect of a territorial base for a monarchical restoration, although at no time, except possibly in the Vendée, did the rebellions have the support of an undivided population. It was always a question of bursts of revolt distributed in a patchwork pattern across the countryside. Why this was so, and why some areas found the policies of the revolutionary regimes so intolerable that they were prepared to rebel while others allowed their grievances to simmer, has exercised the minds both of contemporaries and, ever since, of historians. No single explanation, especially in a country so diverse as France, has ever been wholly satisfactory and it may be futile to look for one. However, one connecting thread may be identified, that is localism, the desire by various communities to defend their customary distinctions from the intrusions of the modern state and its agents. This could act as a unifying force bringing together otherwise widely divergent sources of discontent and aims. Religion was another great unifying element, above all in the South and West, but its place in the popular Counter-Revolution needs to be considered in more detail.

The earliest expression of popular opposition to the Revolution came from the South. The Midi, that is the Provinces of Languedoc and Provence but also including Lyons and the Lyonnais, was a world apart to many Frenchmen, and indeed thought of itself in the same light. Political moderation during the Revolution, or for that matter before it, was not a characteristic of the region, at whatever end of the political spectrum one cares to look. The tradition of the vendetta, personalised and often savage reprisal against one's opponents, was easily translated into the political sphere. The intensity of its sense of provincial separatism, the strong tradition of municipal politics and communal action, and the early polarisation of opinion between Third Estate and the 'privileged' Orders, between rich and poor, had encouraged the growth of political extremism and violence in the region well before the Estates General met.

At least two other factors marked out lower Languedoc, the part of the Midi with the earliest and most prolonged resistance to the Revolution: the economic and the religious. The Department of the Gard, which was to be the centre of counter-revolutionary activity, was a major textile-producing region going through intense change in which the weavers were in the process of being turned from independent producers into dispersed 'factory' workers, that is dependent on a merchant who distributed the materials through agents. The richer merchants were often Protestant. Lower Languedoc was the heartland of French Protestantism and a region with a long tradition of ferocious religious warfare. The last of these had been the Camisard revolt in 1704 but memories of it and the persecutions which had produced it were still alive. The extension to Protestants of full civil equality in 1789, the ecclesiastical decrees by the National Assembly such as the abolition of monasticism and the refusal to accept Catholicism as the religion of the state, all culminating in the Civil Constitution of the Clergy in

June 1790, poured fuel on the smouldering religious, economic and social discontents of the region. The Catholic landowners could now come forward more convincingly as the defenders of the customary rights of the Catholic lower orders.

These alliances of disparate forces were characteristic of the Counter-Revolution, as we have seen in the case of the émigrés. In lower Languedoc Catholic notables and Catholic wage-earners had interests which could not always survive economic change, social suspicion, the conflict of town and country and a great many other sources of tension. Support for Counter-Revolution amongst the peasantry and urban wage-earner never implied acceptance of the *ancien régime* in its entirety. Nevertheless, in the Midi as elsewhere, the intensity of the conflict, the emotions which were aroused and the collective memories they evoked were to obscure these differences, pushing both sides to extremes.

Alarm bells were ringing in the Gard well before the Assembly's religious programme was complete. Scattered riots and protests were given a wider significance by the activities of François Froment, a displaced and vengeful ecclesiastical official, who in January 1790 visited Turin and gained Artois' approval for a plan to capture control of a number of towns throughout the Midi in preparation for an invasion of the South-east by an émigré army. That, of course, was never a possibility although the region remained at the forefront of émigré thinking for many years to come. There were disturbances through much of the Midi and into the South-west during the spring of 1790, some of them involving loss of life, but it was in Nîmes where Froment concentrated his activities and where events were to set their mark on the region until long into the Restoration period. Froment had established his own companies of National Guard to counter the official Protestant-dominated one. The resulting clashes as both sides attempted to win control at the Departmental elections led in June to the Cevenol Protestants answering the appeal for help of their urban co-religionists by pouring into the town and carrying out a slaughter of Catholics. About 300 were killed, Froment himself only narrowly escaping. This *bagarre* (brawl) brought the Protestants to power both in the municipality, from which they had been excluded, and in the Department. Froment, who was to remain a principal link in the counter-revolutionary activities of Languedoc until the Restoration, spent much of that time attempting to restore the Catholic ascendancy which had been lost as a result of the *bagarre*.

In the meantime the shock waves of the events in Nîmes reverberated throughout the region but especially the Gard and the southern part of the neighbouring Ardèche, giving counter-revolutionary leaders a much firmer base on which to operate. Here was evidence that Catholics needed to band together against a Revolution that threatened their very existence. Something like a directing group of Counter-Revolution began to form, of whom the leading pair were brothers, Claude and Dominique Allier. This directing group came to be known as the Camp de Jalès committee after the remote valley in which, in August 1790, a large number of the region's National Guards were called to what appeared a patriotic rally but was, unknown to most of those who turned up, a cover for the organisation of Catholic defence. The committee formed there set about organising an insurrection for February 1791. The whole plan was doomed from the start since it was known to the authorities and had no chance of outside help from the émigrés, whose own schemes for an invasion in the previous December had failed. The result was that this first insurrection was a disaster and the Jalès organisation disintegrated. Hope remained alive in the Allier brothers for a revival of the confederation, and they continued to press the idea on the princes of an insurrection in the Midi which would create a counter-revolutionary stronghold from which, in alliance with foreign troops, an attack could be launched on Lyons and Paris.

Although Claude Allier pressed the scheme on Coblenz with the usual wildly optimistic estimates of the amount of support at his disposal, there was also an element of desperation in it all. The Catholic royalist alliance was showing strains as economic pressures at the beginning of 1792 drew Protestant and Catholic worker together while in the countryside also religious antagonisms were temporarily forgotten in widespread attacks on the remnants of the seigneurial system. It was the emergence, briefly, of that pattern of conflict between rich and poor which had been familiar in much of the rest of France but had been overlaid in Languedoc by the peculiarities of its religious and economic composition. It was not the last time that such resentments broke through to threaten the leadership of the notables, whether Protestant bourgeois or Catholic gentry. The Alliers were trying to stage a rising before the ground crumbled beneath them.

The princes were persuaded to give the planned insurrection their support. It was a complete disaster. The various groups were riddled with jealousies which led to some premature risings. The two commanders appointed by the princes fell out with each other. The one who was sent into the region, Saillans, seriously overestimated his support, rushed the preparations and in June was easily defeated and captured by the government forces. That, apart from one small rising the next year, was the end of open insurrection in the Midi for some years to come.

Lower Languedoc and the Midi in general did not cease to be a centre of royalist hopes and conspiracies. Men like Froment were irreconcilable and their hands were to be evident behind many of the disturbances in future years, the White Terror of 1795 for example, and its successors in 1814 and 1815. There was a remarkable continuity to the enmities of the region. But in 1792–4 these either dried up or were diverted into other channels of discontent. As Catholic and Protestant small merchant and artisan drew together, impelled largely by economic distress, the wealthier Protestant bourgeoisie who had been in the forefront of political activity since 1789 pulled back in alarm at events locally and nationally. Their involvement in the 'federalist' revolt, mild though it was in Nîmes at least, was to cost them dearly when the Terror arrived in the Gard early in 1794. Neither could the peasants be consistently relied upon by the opponents of the Revolution. The deeper grievances and disappointments, a sense of betrayed hope, which impelled and to a great extent unified the peasantry of the West, were not to be found in Lower Languedoc. Religion also acted as a disunifying force in Languedoc. There was none of what has been called the 'moral homogeneity' which is to be found among the peasantry of the West and which made Counter-Revolution there such a formidable and enduring force.

That is not to say that the Revolution attracted any very deep loyalty even in the apparently patriot circles of the Midi. On the other hand, too much need not be read into the commitment of counter-revolutionaries. As Jolivet observes, cries of 'long live the king' were 'less a profession of political faith than an expression of discontent, a protest against measures which hurt their deepest feelings or damaged their material interests'. On the whole the countryside wanted to be left alone, a wish that revolutionary governments, unlike those of the *ancien régime*, were unable to accept. Counter-revolutionary conspirators like Froment could feed on the resentments that this provoked but they relied to a great extent on stoking up old enmities and partly for this reason could never count on a unified and homogeneous peasant population such as in many parts of the West.

That is by no means to underestimate the potential threat the South could have posed to the Revolution had foreign powers been able, and willing, to act more in concert with each other. It was far more accessible than the West and strategically more important. The key to much of it was Lyons, a city which figured prominently in almost all counter-revolutionary schemes for much of the earlier part of the Revolution. That was mainly because of its closeness to the frontier, the ease of access which made it possible for agents to slip in and out, its attraction to various disaffected elements fleeing from the disorders of the countryside, and the considerable tensions to which it had been subject from the very earliest stages of the Revolution. After 1793 it was to become the 'capital of the Counter-Revolution' but the groundwork for that distinction had been laid in 1790 when the émigrés made it the centre of their grandiose plots of that year. The chief planner of Lyons' part was its former first *échevin* (or mayor) Imbert-Colomès, rich, recently ennobled, and a *parlementaire* royalist who in September was made by Artois his sole representative in the area. He had already failed in an effort to create separate National Guard companies in the city and the plan in December to seize and hold it pending the arrival of the princes also failed. That did nothing to diminish the importance of the city in counter-revolutionary thinking: 'once the princes are in control of this town', Imbert wrote to Coblenz in the spring of 1792, 'they will control the entire South'.

Imbert's hopes appeared to have been brought closer with the outbreak in 1793 of the 'federalist' revolts. These revolts were not a part of the Counter-Revolution but quarrels within the Revolution itself. Nevertheless they were to have consequences for counter-revolutionary activity above all in Lyons. In addition part of the origins of federalism lay in the same strong sense of offended provincial identity, of separateness from the North and Paris, which can be found lying behind the clearly counter-revolutionary insurrections elsewhere. In itself that was not sufficient to sustain a strong federalist movement; it needed to be supported by the deep social divisions which existed in Lyons, Marseilles and Toulon which were able to break the control of the wealthy notables who had dominated the revolutions in those cities. The 'federalist' revolts were attempts by the wealthier elites to recapture control.

These were not royalist uprisings although the Convention labelled them as such for propaganda purposes; but they easily became linked with some frankly counter-revolutionary elements as violence and denunciation pushed the two sides to extremes. Lyons chose as its commander a declared royalist, the comte de Précy, although he did take an oath of loyalty to the Republic (for which 'pure' royalists never quite forgave him). Other royalists like Imbert were coming out into the open as well, while by necessity many officers were monarchists. Much the same pattern took shape in Marseilles which went as far as an act of religious expiation for having accepted the fall of the monarchy. The federalists of Toulon were forced to accept not just royalist officers but also an alliance with the British Admiral Hood in the name of the monarchy and to declare Louis XVII king.

The Midi remained a problem for revolutionary governments, a prey to brigandage, swelled by deserters from the army and economic hardship, the recurring problem of religious conflict and the paying-off of old scores, and the fact that the whole region remained at the centre of many royalist conspiracies. None of this was helped by the representatives sent out by the Convention to cleanse the Midi. Even when they were southerners themselves, such as Fréron and Barras, they saw the whole region as beyond redemption. The resulting harsh and insensitive punishments hardened attitudes; Lyons in particular became notorious as the scene of Fouché and Collot's draconian measures, above all the mass shootings known as the *mitraillades*. Partly as a result of this, as well as the trampling on its sensibilities by the importation of outsiders to take charge, it continued to lie at the heart of counter-revolutionary manoeuvres. Its strategic position accounted for some of this as well but the destruction of the centre and the resulting ruins increased the facility it had always offered in its narrow streets of finding somewhere to hide.

Before the federalist revolts had even broken out a more serious rising had been raging in the West. In the long run it was to be far more permanent in its consequences. This revolt, misleadingly but conveniently known as the Vendéan, has tended to attract more attention from historians than the earlier, and potentially more dangerous, risings in the Midi. There are very good reasons for this, if only because contemporaries also paid it more attention, the analysis of its causes has itself become a part of the historical debate on the Revolution, and it was to mark for over a century the map of political attitudes in France, a constant reminder of its scale and intensity.

The west of France had been subject to outbreaks of violence, increasing in scale, for about two years before the general rising which broke out in early March 1793 in most of Brittany, lower Anjou,

Poitou and Maine, provoked by the application in the region of the law of the previous month ordering a levy of 300,000 men for the war effort. North of the Loire the rising was rapidly contained and broke up into the series of irregular skirmishes and ambushes known as *chouannerie*. South of the Loire the pattern was very different. Here, a full-scale war was allowed to develop and the outline emerged of organised armies which were able to overwhelm the small towns, capture Saumur and Angers and lay siege to Nantes where the rebels were checked in late June. Thereafter, they were slowly, if unevenly, to be driven from their main points until, in October, a devastating defeat at Cholet turned into an ill-defined effort by the rebels to capture a Channel port. Their failure to achieve this at Granville in Normandy was followed by a ragged retreat back to the Loire and their destruction at Savenay in December. Irregular warfare both north and south of the Loire was to last until 1796, with a serious if brief outbreak in 1799, and a complete pacification only with the advent of Napoleon. There were to be lesser insurrections in 1815 and 1832.

The scale and severity of these risings, the fact that they seemed to represent the massive rejection of the Revolution by a whole countryside, and the continuity of attitudes that they left behind, has produced an extensive literature on their causes. Many contemporaries, and those who lived in the immediate aftermath of the rebellions, were in little doubt as to what had happened, although there were a number who sounded notes of caution along with a more sophisticated analysis. But for the general run of republicans it was the result of a conspiracy by the aristocracy and priesthood which had led a simple and gullible people astray. Only this could account for the inexplicable hostility of the peasantry to a revolution which was in their interests. Contemporaries sympathetic to the revolt, as well as conservative historians, placed the initiative more clearly with the peasantry, seeing the role of the aristocracy and Church simply as an illustration of the close bonds of piety and affection which united the different strands of rural society in a common cause against an impious revolution. Here, in the West, suggested many aristocratic recollections, was something of a golden age of rustic harmony: a resident seigneur joining in the sports and pastimes of his tenantry and occasionally admitting them to his own; a respectful but sturdy and independent-minded peasantry, all at one in their devotion to King and Church. More modern interpretations have accepted the popular base of the risings but, as in the case of the Midi, have concentrated to a greater extent on the economic condition of the region, the contrasts of wealth and poverty, the Revolution's role in the development of administrative uniformity, the varieties of landholding, and the relations between town and country with which all these were involved. Finally, the religious element, which all contemporaries of whatever political persuasion saw as fundamental, has continued to find its place in all assessments of the insurrection. Again as in the Midi, none of these factors excludes the others: at various stages all can be found playing some part. '*Chouannerie*', claims Reinhard, 'was a coalition of interests and convictions hurt or rebuffed by the new order. Trying to explain it by a single cause makes it unintelligible and impossible to understand its persistence.'

The nineteenth-century West was so clearly distinct in political and religious terms from the rest of France that it was easy to read these distinctions back into the eighteenth century. How far this can be done with safety is a major problem in analysing the causes of the insurrection. In another respect at least there is no problem: the landscape was distinctive. The West had a characteristic countryside of small enclosed fields, dense hedgerows on top of high embankments, numerous small woods and streams which became raging torrents after rain, and sunken roads or lanes, frequently impassable in winter and difficult even in summer. Scattered across this *bocage*, the term for this type of landscape, were hamlets and isolated farmsteads. Within the insurrectionary zone itself, that is south of the Loire in the part of southern Anjou known as the Mauges and in the northern districts of the Vendée and Deux-Sèvres, towns were relatively few and tended to be scattered around the edges. The *bocage* caused republican generals many difficulties and although they naturally liked to make much of their problems they had a point: the mechanised armies of 1944 were also to have difficulties. But many other areas were as suited for guerrilla warfare, much of the Midi for example, and, crucially, by no means all of the *bocage* joined the Counter-Revolution or even sympathised with it. There were many examples of 'republican *bocage*'. The terrain simply made it more difficult to deal with the revolt once it had occurred. Yet this brings us to the central problem: why did areas so alike in appearance, so geographically close, respond in such totally different ways as communities to the Revolution?

The revolts in the West had some clear and immediate causes such as excessive demands for tax contributions, military service and much else in return for the poor rewards of the Revolution. The Revolution, however, also has to be set in the context of the changes in the countryside, in its relationship with the towns, the expansion of central government, and the impact of this on customary patterns of rural life. *Ancien régime* governments, at least in the eighteenth century, had largely left the countryside alone. The wrath of the peasantry had been directed against its local agents rather than the central government which remained a distant and unseen force. Those agents were the more resented in that they were likely to be drawn from the class which seemed to present the real threat to the rural community, the lawyer and other representatives of urban cultural and commercial values. This was not new. Complaints that old institutions and relationships, usually enshrined in the seigneurie, were being bought up and distorted for commercial gain, can be found in the sixteenth century. Indeed, in many regions the seigneurie which was the base of much of the order and cohesion of the countryside was in an advanced stage of disintegration. Yet this was by no means so everywhere. Much remained and where it did the seigneur was still the 'first inhabitant' and the machinery of the seigneurie had a useful function. The peasant's complaints against the seigneur did not necessarily mean that he sought the abolition of the institution.

Penetrating into this world from the town came the lawyer, the villain of rural life. Superior, literate, knowing, be-wigged, he seemed a constant reminder of the undervalued merits of agriculture, of which contemporary literature was so full. Yet the relationship between town and country was a complex one: in many respects they complemented and depended on each other for markets, employment, expertise and so on. Neither was there necessarily much resentment over urban purchases of land. It had been going on for too long. The nub of the matter was a clash of values between the commercial, official, free-thinking, condescending urban world and the traditional strengths of the countryside. Rural resentments were likely to be strongest where urban penetration was weakest, that is, less well-established.

This is the central thesis of the study of southern Anjou by Charles Tilly. He contrasted the heart of the insurrectionary zone, the Mauges, with the area immediately to its east, the Saumurois, which had long-standing commercial contacts through the wine trade, an 'urbanised' countryside, good communications which made it open and receptive to outside influences, while the bourgeoisie was seen as an associate rather than a competitor of the rural world. The Mauges, on the other hand, was only in the early stages of the penetration of urban influences, cut off by its remoteness from large towns, poor communications and subsistence agriculture. The substantial number of weavers, outworkers dependent on the Cholet kerchief manufacture which had grown rapidly in the later part of the century, identified their interests with the surrounding rural community with which they remained in close touch. They were not, therefore, an instrument of rural modernisation and were to be found on the insurrectionary side in 1793 in the same proportions as the peasants.

Another work, of equal importance to Tilly's: Paul Bois' *Paysans de l'Ouest* (1960) also studies an area of western France, the Sarthe, where, as in southern Anjou, there was a marked contrast between the 'patriot' East and the *chouan* West of the Department. In the West Bois identified a prosperous and ambitious peasantry leasing land from a usually absentee nobility which owned about 20 per cent of the usually large properties. Here, the main rivals to the peasants' ambitions were the bourgeoisie from the local small towns. In the eastern part of the Department, on the other hand, a poorer peasantry was unable to compete with the bourgeoisie for land. However, in contrast to the Mauges, an extensive textile industry with its large number of weavers employed on the usual outwork basis linked the rural population with the towns and the bourgeoisie in a common economic interest as well as opening out contacts with the wider world. Town and country were partners sharing common interests and assumptions. The weavers reinforced this pattern rather than being themselves an instrument of the modernisation of the countryside. In the Mauges, as in the western Sarthe, what Bois has called the 'moral homogeneity' of the rural population, so essential for the success of the revolt, had not yet been undermined by the successful intrusion of different values emanating from the towns. Where those values were well-entrenched or where the urban-based authorities were able to act swiftly and in overwhelming force as along the Loire, near seaports or good roads, the Revolution was either welcomed or met with only feeble resistance.

The argument, therefore, for seeing the rejection of the Revolution in many parts of rural France as a reflection of the degree to which the countryside had already been modernised through urban influences is a strong one. But many problems remain in the way of seeing it as the key which somehow will resolve all difficulties. Too many exceptions and contradictions remain: in the Gard, for example, where the market-orientated silk-weavers and peasant owner-occupiers of the

Catholic districts of the Cévennes could still be found on the side of Counter-Revolution; or in the Nord, the most commercialised region of France, where responses to the Revolution were complex and often social in motivation rather than clearly economic. Neither is it entirely clear that the peasantry resented the towns as such, even though their spleen was to be vented on them during the Revolution; it was the bureaucratic and legal aspects of the towns which they sought out for punishment, not the urban population. The distinction can be seen in the traditional forms of punishment dealt out by the rebels when they captured the towns: the burning of records was usual. That had a material and symbolic aspect: material in that tax records usually went up in flames; symbolic in that the written document represented legal control, the power of the educated over the rural world.

These traditional forms of protest are a reminder that the conflict of urban and rural values was not new but was sharpened by a Revolution which did so much to reinforce the former. That reinforcement of the urban element in the countryside was especially resented because the Revolution had appeared to offer opportunities to rural elites, clergy and richer peasants for example, to take administrative control of their communities. Thus many lower clergy became mayors in the early stages. In fact, they failed to hold on to these positions against the electoral tactics of the towns. This may have been all the more galling in that most of the towns of the West (with a handful of exceptions) were tiny, tolerated by the surrounding peasantry because they provided necessary services. Their new pretensions were, to say the least, irritating. The savagery of the Vendéan conflict is in many respects best seen as a clash over rival values in which each side felt it was threatened. The intrusion into the countryside of new, commercially based relationships is one aspect of this, and another is the administrative incursions just described; but both are unsatisfactory as complete arguments.

Another aspect which encapsulated the clash of values at the heart of so much of the Counter-Revolution was the religious policy of the revolutionary governments. All contemporaries, of whatever political persuasion, agreed that religion had a central place in the revolts in the West. The region, with important exceptions, was to reject the Civil Constitution of the Clergy on a massive scale. In all the insurrectionary zones the refusal to take the oath was overwhelming: about 90 per cent in Cholet District, 88 per cent in Saint-Florent-le-Vieil, 75 per cent in Vihiers, compared to a roughly even division in the neighbouring

Saumurois. In Brittany 83 per cent refused the oath in Ille-et-Vilaine, in Vannes only one out of 67 rectors and vicars although just thirty miles along the coast at Lorient all 54 took it. The insurrection became something of a religious crusade, defence of their religion appearing to the peasants the main purpose of the rebellion. That was also how it appeared to most contemporaries and for very good reasons. Almost all the symbols of the revolt, especially the Sacred Heart which was worn as its badge, and whatever pronouncements were made about its purpose, gave a prominent place to religion. Ultimately a greater sensitivity to religious feeling was to be one of the keys to bringing the insurrection to an end. Neither can there be any doubt of the central part of the Church in the life of the countryside everywhere in France and in the West possibly more than elsewhere. The Church had a fundamental role in the social life of a settlement pattern such as was to be found in the West, a role unchallenged by the sort of lay religious societies to be found in many other parts of France, especially in the South. In a region of scattered communities and isolated farms the local church was the main social link: it brought the community together on Sundays and festivals, its spire was the visible symbol of its identity, its bells the audible rallying signal, marking out the day, as well as the religious and social high-points of family and communal life.

On the other hand, all rural societies were to some degree religious and the Church played a central role in their lives, lives which were after all governed by the inexplicable and often devastating vagaries of nature. The priest was expected to give meaning to these, to provide a framework for the peasant's life and, usually to his distaste, sanctify some of the frankly pagan customs of the parish. It is therefore hardly surprising that popular Counter-Revolution everywhere had its religious dimension. But that is not by any means to see religion as a cause. The main problem is to assess the extent to which the West was different in religious terms from its rural counterparts elsewhere. In the nineteenth century it undoubtedly was: a sharply defined 'confessional' line marked it off from a more sceptical and anti-clerical Centre and East. The difficulty lies in the extent to which this was a product of the revolt or pre-dated the Revolution.

Almost all recent historians have seen the religious element as a reflection of social and economic discontents rather than as an independent factor in the revolt. The Civil Constitution of the Clergy and the oath it required became in a sense a 'referendum' on a

Revolution which for the peasantry of the West and elsewhere had already failed. The priesthood of the disaffected areas followed either willingly or under pressure the opinions of their parishioners. There is, however, a very strong argument for modifying this view. It has been put with some force over a number of years by Timothy Tackett.

Tackett argues that the 'West' (in the sense of the counter-revolutionary regions rather than the geographical ones) was clearly distinct in a number of ways from its neighbours and that the activities of the authorities made these differences more acute. There were more country priests and their assistants in the West than elsewhere in France and this enabled them to live in small communities or 'micro-societies' resisting absorption into the secular values of the surrounding community. They were therefore able to insist on the high spiritual values set out by the Counter-Reformation and to demonstrate them in their personal lives. In addition, Counter-Reformation emphasis on the value of symbols and display was adapted to peasant practice, to the processions and festivals of rural life. Elsewhere, particularly in the Paris Basin, the solitary priest became all too easily the secular-minded 'citizen-priest' so fashionable among eighteenth-century rationalists.

The parish clergy in the West was also better off financially than in much of the rest of France: the modestly paid *congruiste* (that is, given a fixed sum) was relatively rare. The priest was often, on the contrary, a substantial man of property yet aroused no resentment from his parishioners because the tithe was seen to be going to someone whose prestige was high and whose status as spiritual leader of his flock was unquestioned. He was also a man who was likely to be not just local, which was by no means unusual outside central France, but rural in background, belonging to the richer peasantry who were the opinion leaders in the countryside. The parish priest therefore understood his parishioners, all the more because he was usually long-serving in the parish, and shared many of their attitudes, especially their resentment of the town and its values. A 'cultural dichotomy' between an anti-clerical, radical, urban society and a devout countryside was particularly strong in the future *chouan* areas of the West. The imposition of the oath accepting the Civil Constitution of the Clergy at the end of 1790 could therefore be regarded as an assault on a 'priest-orientated belief system'.

There is some evidence from other parts of France which supports much of this. Features of the French Church normally associated with the nineteenth century can, probably not surprisingly, be found making their appearance in the eighteenth. The 'confessional line', for example, dividing devout from anti-clerical areas can be found between the pays de Bray and the pays de Caux in Normandy, the former being 'bad' (in a religious sense) and the latter 'good' in both the eighteenth and nineteenth centuries. The drift towards a more secular attitude can be found already in Provence before the Revolution. There is also a marked trend in much of the country towards an increase in the recruitment of priests from the countryside and from lower social levels, a pattern which was a marked feature of the nineteenth-century Church in France.

There remain, however, major points of doubt in the way of arguing for a pre-existing pattern of distinctive religious devotion in the West: too many of the features described above can also be found elsewhere. The clergy of the West, for example, were probably better provided for financially than elsewhere, but the poor parish priest was anyway much rarer than legend and contemporary fashionable belief would have it. These things are of course relative but the priest was normally among the more substantial citizens of the parish and in many areas very well off indeed. Again, long service in a parish was the custom. Once a benefice was obtained, perhaps in his thirties, it was a risky matter for a priest to abandon it in the hope of something better. There were many compensations in the life of a country priest even if it was not always the rural idyll of an increasing amount of fiction. Staying thirty or forty, even fifty, years in the same parish was by no means uncommon. Outside the Paris region, it was normal for priests to be natives of the diocese, even sometimes of the district, in which they held a parish. They inevitably came to know their parishioners better than anyone else. Everywhere in France the relationship of the clergy with their flocks was complex and spiritual example was no guarantee of amicable or respectful relationships. The attempts by a priesthood, whose quality was generally rising, to elevate the moral and spiritual condition of their charges meant an almost constant round of battle against the standards of rural life, against what one priest called 'baptised idolaters'. Respect and affection for their priest was by no means uncommon but that did not preclude asserting the claims, material and customary, of the village when necessary; neither did it mean following the leadership of the priest automatically, although, as suggested above, it may be that in the West and similar regions the clergy had been more sensitive and understanding in their attitude to the 'folklorique' customs of the countryside.

A great many influences led a priest in 1790–1 to decide for or against taking the oath: his fellow priests, his bishop, his seminary, even, possibly, the extent to which the diocese had been affected by the theological movement known as Jansenism. There were also material considerations – how far the Revolution improved his financial position. Of course, this was less likely to be the case in areas where the clergy was well off. But most of all, there was the influence of his parishoners. What the peasantry were not interested in were the finer points of theological detail which perplexed even the clergy. The 'constitutional' Church regarded itself as entirely orthodox and Catholic. This was not a delusion: there was no change in doctrine or any interference in that direction by the state. That is one reason why so many of the constitutional clergy sent into the rebel areas were bewildered at their treatment. It is also why many patriot parishes could see no problem in retaining a refractory priest. The pays de Caux, mentioned above, was a region with a large majority of refractory priests yet, unlike its Norman neighbours to the south, Counter-Revolution made little headway. What we may be dealing with here is not simply a matter of religious doctrine, an assault on faith, but another aspect of that intrusion into the affairs of the countryside by 'alien' elements, urban in their attitudes and possibly backgrounds, just as in the case of the administrations which were set up from 1790. The urban-elected constitutional priests were no different in doctrinal terms but they represented a different style, that of the more rationalist, severe, priest of central France, less sympathetic to the devotional styles of the West and its priests. In fact, many old attitudes and antagonisms surfaced during the turmoil of 1790–1, much of which had little to do with religion. It may reflect, it has been argued, a traditional element of insubordination in some parishes and obedience in others; just as rivalries between parishes could be reflected in opposing attitudes to the Oath.

The religious element is, therefore, inescapable and significant but its role as a prime mover in the insurrection must be treated with caution. In some respects its place may be far more important than that. It became, in a society under stress, an affirmation of cultural identity, of mutual cohesion, drawing together communities under threat and giving a moral dimension to what might otherwise seem mundanely material grievances. Clergy and community could come together, perhaps for different reasons, but both against a morally, spiritually and culturally destructive Revolution enforced by unsympathetic urban outsiders without any compensating material gains. It helped to create a separate identity for the rebel West which gave the insurrection a wholly different character, a wider scale, and left a permanent imprint on the region.

Therefore it is no longer possible to reduce the force of religion to a simple supporting role but we do need to turn back to the social, economic and political sources of the rebellion for a fuller explanation. The peasantry in the West, as elsewhere, had large expectations of the Revolution and it was widely welcomed. Some future *chouan* areas saw a high incidence of chateaux-burning in 1789 and 1791; there was a high rate of participation in the local elections by the peasantry of the Western Sarthe; a great many parish clergy were to serve in the new administrations set up by the National Assembly. But by at least 1791 something had clearly happened to turn this early favourable response sour and a substantial part of the peasantry had become deeply disappointed with what the Revolution had to offer. They felt themselves, in Petitfrère's expression, 'the victims of a swindle'.

The key to this, Le Goff and Sutherland have claimed, lies in the structure of rural society in the West. To a varying extent it was a region of lease-holders rather than owner-occupiers. This was most clearly the case in the Mauges where the peasantry, although constituting nearly three-quarters of the cultivators, owned only about 17 per cent of the land compared to the nobility's 60 per cent and roughly 17 per cent by the bourgeoisie. Peasant ownership was higher in upper Brittany, at about one-third, but here the situation was complicated by a form of lease known as *domaine congéable* which gave the tenant the freehold of the buildings but not the land. The distinctive feature of much of the West was that the more prosperous and substantial peasants, the opinion leaders of rural society, were tenants. This special place was the more marked because the nobility, outside a few areas, was very largely absentee. Indeed, in Brittany farmers of this type had a traditional role as leaders in conflicts with the seigneur. At the same time, the tenant farmers were not so wealthy as to distance themselves from the mass of the rural population. There was a broadly diffused, if modest, wealth, stability of employment and tenure, some sense of general responsibility for the poor and a reasonably self-contained economy with only limited market contacts, all helping to promote that 'moral homogeneity' referred to earlier. The significance of this is again illustrated in the pays de Caux where a greater diversity of rural wealth meant a less unified countryside and where the better-off peasant generally did well out of the Revolution.

This was not the case in the insurrectionary zones. Many of the expectations of its peasantry were much the same as elsewhere: the relief of poverty, the reform of the seigneurial system and of the tithe, a more equitable tax assessment, abolition of militia service. But in a region so dominated by lease-holders a transfer of ownership, or at least reform of the lease structure, held a high place, particularly since the balance of advantage had tipped against the tenant farmer in the 1780s and in favour of the landowner as rents outstripped prices. Yet from the beginning the National Assembly and the local administrations threw their influence on the side of property, the landowner rather than the tenant. The Decrees of 4 August 1789, though promising to 'abolish the feudal regime in its entirety', in practice designated many dues, even some personal ones, as property which had to be bought out. The result was to perpetuate the wrangling over dues and contribute to the continuation of attacks on chateaux which had so disturbed the countryside in the summer of 1789. The intervention by National Guards to protect the property of threatened seigneurs caused many of the inhabitants to feel betrayed by those urban bourgeois interests which in 1788 in Brittany had sought their help in their struggles against the Breton aristocracy.

The tithe was a more contentious issue than seigneurial dues, which were quite light in the West. Its suppression in April 1790 appeared unambiguous enough but in the following December a decree allowed it to be added to the rents. The principal beneficiaries were therefore the landowners, not the tenants. They thus frequently found themselves worse off as a result of the changes. An even greater source of irritation in Brittany was the slowness of the Assembly to deal with the lease-hold system, *domaine congéable*, which tenants wished to convert into ownership. The Assembly was sensitive to any possible limitation or attack upon property and so, when it did decree on the issue in August 1791, and again in the following year, it stopped a long way short of peasant demands. By that time the peasantry in large areas of Brittany had lost interest in a Revolution which had done so little for them. The exceptions were the areas where owner-occupiers predominated.

The fundamental source of grievance therefore was the failure of the revolutionary governments, locked into a rigid attitude towards what constituted property, to satisfy the long-term aspirations of the leading elements of peasant society in the West. Other grievances added fuel to this but were probably not in themselves enough to provoke revolt. The sales of Church lands in the West as everywhere favoured the bourgeoisie but tended simply to confirm the existing shape of land-holding and a well-established pattern of purchase stretching back for some centuries. The increased tax burden imposed by the Revolution was no doubt more serious. Where the Assembly did meet the demands in the *cahiers* for relief it often made the situation worse, for example by abolishing the salt tax, the *gabelle*. Brittany had in any case been exempt from this, besides which it was simply added to general taxation. The salt smugglers who had flourished in the Breton borderlands were to be prominent in *chouannerie*. An increased tax burden everywhere was made even less bearable by the grain requisitions, price controls, pressures to enrol in the National Guard and other exhortations to revolutionary zeal, the whole finally capped by conscription in a cause for which few peasants felt any enthusiasm at all.

In the early days of the Revolution some priests and nobles had seen service on the new municipalities as the means through which they could establish their authority in the countryside and resist the intrusion of outside elements. In the case of the clergy it offered the opportunity to carry through that 'moralisation' of society so important to the eighteenth-century Church. But by 1791–2 clergy and nobility were rarely to be found in the local authorities. The administrations had been largely captured, to the bitter resentment of the clergy especially, by urban and bourgeois elements. These were now responsible for the revolutionary changes in the Church. In some areas they carried out their task with a degree of sympathy and understanding as a result of which trouble was avoided but all too often the interventions in the countryside by the authorities were carried out in brutal fashion on behalf of property-owners by National Guards, again usually townsmen. As the administration in the countryside disintegrated and the supporters of the Revolution appeared as a beleaguered minority, those interventions became even more frequent and took on the form of punitive expeditions into alien and hostile territory.

The application of the Civil Constitution of the Clergy required even more delicacy than the other measures, especially the task of bringing into the countryside the new Constitutional clergy, the nominees of the urban administrations, bringing with them, not new doctrines, but certainly a new style of worship. That it could be handled successfully is shown, for example, in the Moselle, in eastern France, where many non-jurors were allowed to remain as late as September 1792 and in some cases even longer. In the West the implementation of the Civil Constitution had all the appearance of an invasion, the violation of a community's identity, reinforced by such measures as the abolition of parishes in communities of less than 6000 inhabitants and the subsequent removal of bells and records. The entry of the new priest, the *intru*, into his church was often followed by a ritual cleansing of the building by the inhabitants. The opposition to the Revolution acquired an ideological base which could cut across material interest and class differences. It reinforced the identification of the Revolution with injustice, tyranny and godlessness and strengthened, in areas like the Mauges, the sense of an embattled rural community fighting against those outside who sought to subvert its traditions. Consequently the insurrection was to have many of the features of a crusade in its symbols, its ferocity, its hysteria, outbursts of vision-sightings and pilgrimages. The non-juring Church and its faithful in the West took to the open fields just as the Protestants of the Cévennes had done from the end of the seventeenth century. And just as the revolt of the Camisards can be seen as the Protestant response to what has been called the 'deculturisation' of the community, provoking an explosion of mass emotion capable of sustaining a long and savage war, so also in the West there are precisely the same elements of a defensive war against a cultural invasion.

There are, then, no neat universal causes of popular Counter-Revolution. Regions of predominant lease-holding can be found which remain 'patriot', just as many 'refractory' regions do. Relationships with the town, 'openness' to the outside world, communications, proximity to the frontier, the sensitivity or otherwise of local authorities, all these in varying proportions played their part but none is decisive in determining the response of a region to the Revolution. In the Vendée the various factors which might form the material for revolt were all present in greater numbers than elsewhere and were balanced by fewer of the elements which might have checked an insurrection. One factor among them all was, however, critical: the government needed to make an early and effective reply to disturbances. This meant ample numbers of troops close at hand. In the Vendée this was not the case. The government lost control at the beginning. That control was already under severe strain long before the full-scale rebellion broke out: by the beginning of 1792 administration had all but collapsed in rural areas while the level of violence was such that constitutional priests showed a reluctance to serve there and the administrators took refuge in the towns from which they sallied forth from time to time under the protection of the National Guard. There were major outbreaks of violence in the course of 1792, of which the most serious was an attack on Chatillon by 6000 peasants in August. The insurrection therefore scarcely fell upon unsuspecting authorities but its speed and extent, involving about ten Departments, caught them unprepared in all but a few areas. In southern Anjou the revolt was allowed to develop into full-scale warfare.

By the middle of 1793, then, the external Counter-Revolution could take comfort in the existence, at the least, of widespread disaffection with the Revolution over much of France, outright revolt in the West, and an apparently sound base of support in the South, while Lyons, the key to so much of the region, appeared to be open for royalist control. But bringing all these strands together was quite another matter not just because of problems of geographical separation, of accurate information, of supply, but because they were genuinely popular movements with their own origins, leadership and motives. Popular royalism was to prove itself vastly different from the variety practised in the emigration.

3

The Emigration and the Allies

The entry of Britain into the war against the French in February 1793 shifted the whole focus of the exterior Counter-Revolution's efforts to secure allies. Britain became the mainstay of the alliances against revolutionary and Napoleonic France, and the paymaster of the continental war. The princes were therefore increasingly obliged to look to Britain for help and to give way, reluctantly, to the principles on which its policies were based.

The principles and aims of British policy were remarkably clear and consistent right down to Waterloo (and for that matter beyond) even if the execution and means were sometimes confused and inept. From the beginning of the Revolution the British government had done its best to remain aloof, welcoming the confusion in France as a means of checking its rival's pretensions. It also had, in common with almost all other observers, a low opinion of the émigrés – 'a contre-revolution must be made of sterner stuff', said the British minister at the Hague. Consequently all appeals for British help were firmly resisted, including those from Whigs like Burke who saw it as a moral issue, while Pitt looked forward confidently to twenty years of peace. The invasion of Belgium by the French after Valmy introduced a more dangerous dimension, even more so after the declaration in November 1792 of the doctrine of 'natural frontiers' and an offer of assistance to all peoples who wished to 'recover their liberty'. The extension in December of the French paper currency, the assignat, to Belgium seemed confirmation of the impending annexation of the country, a threat to traditional British interests in the Low Countries.

Britain therefore went to war to defend its interests and restore a stable balance of power in Europe. That might or might not mean a monarchy in France. This was a view shared by almost all other European powers whose commitment to a monarchy was frequently fitful. What mattered was a stable government which was acceptable to the French people. Its form was irrelevant as long as it provided the conditions of stability within France and security for Europe. The means to achieving this end varied but in 1793–4 the main thrust of British activity was towards depriving France of the economic bases of war, which were identified as its colonial possessions. In addition Britain paid subsidies to its allies for a continental campaign while providing nominal forces itself. That all made sense from the British point of view and was not without success in capturing some rich prizes in the French West Indies in the spring of 1794. But it aroused the resentment of continental allies like Austria who saw themselves bearing the burden of war in Europe for scant reward while the British advanced their commercial interests. It was to be a factor in the weakening of the first Coalition. As for the princes, it was yet another confirmation, as they saw it, of the selfishly materialistic and predatory approach of Britain towards France, one reason why some of them preferred to look to Spain, a 'family friend', for help.

What Pitt and his political allies resolutely tried to avoid was any involvement in the sort of moral crusade which people like Burke saw in the counter-revolutionary cause, although at times, for domestic reasons, they were unable to resist partially conceding. Nevertheless, quite apart from the poor impression the princes made on them, the British government was impervious to the appeal to join the cause of monarchical solidarity. The important point was to find the best means of achieving the objective of a stable, peaceful France and a secure balance in Europe. Linking British policy to the émigré princes was not necessarily one of those means. Artois' efforts to secure a meeting with George III in May 1793 were a failure and he had to return to Hamm before his creditors caught up with him. On the news of the execution of Louis XVI, Provence declared himself regent, and Artois lieutenant-general. But neither Britain nor Austria felt under any obligation to recognise this. Britain was unwilling to accept a position which would give Provence equal status with other European rulers and so tie British hands as the regime best suited to its objectives. Similarly, when in August 1793 Toulon revolted against the Convention and allowed the British and Spanish fleets into its harbour, Provence was refused permission by the British to go to the city as regent because this might give him equal ally status. As late as the spring of 1794 Dundas, the Home Secretary, asserted that 'the government is in no way committed to the restoration of a monarchical regime in France'. All this reinforced a natural predilection in Provence to see Spain as the most useful ally although Artois, albeit with distaste, recognised the greater resources available in Britain.

British principles were, therefore, unchanging but the methods were entirely pragmatic – a feature which was not readily understood by its allies. During 1794 British strategy underwent the first of its many changes of course. The reconstruction of Pitt's ministry gave greater weight to those who saw the war in moral terms and who wanted to recognise the regency of Provence and assist internal subversion. At the same time the impending collapse of the coalition, as well as the poor performance of the British armies on the Continent, made an alternative strategy attractive. The British government began to develop a policy of encouraging and assisting internal revolt, providing an expeditionary force of émigrés to make a landing, and from within this territorial base allowing Provence to persuade the French of the desirability of a restored monarchy.

But what sort of monarchy? Here we need to unravel yet another strand of the politics of the emigration to set alongside that of the princes and the aristocracy. No group of people stood higher in the demonology of 'pure' royalists than those who had been involved in the framing of the constitutional monarchy. If suspicion and even hatred was intense enough between the princes and their supporters on the one hand and the agents of the Tuileries on the other, it could reach a pitch of frenzy when it came to denouncing those who were indifferently, and somewhat inaccurately, referred to as 'constitutionals' or '*monarchiens*'. They came to be used as terms to describe anyone who had been a member of the Constituent Assembly and had supported the idea of a monarchy limited by an elected, normally two-chamber, assembly defined by property, rather than by the system of Estates General, provincial Estates and *parlements*. People like d'Antraigues made even Breteuil fit into the all-purpose term of abuse, although some included Calonne as well, perhaps with a little more justification.

Like so many of the quarrels of the Counter-Revolution and emigration it had almost as much to do with what had preceded the Revolution as with the Revolution itself. *Monarchien* was meant to describe those like Mounier who in 1789 had voted for a two-chamber Assembly and an absolute veto for the Crown. By 1791, when the term was coined by the Jacobin left, it had come to be used by the 'pures' as an all-embracing term of abuse for constitutional monarchists. Since the numbers were never very large the vitriolic abuse by the 'pures' looks less than rational. In fact it was perfectly so even if the fire was badly aimed. The *monarchiens* were blamed for having started the slide into Revolution. They might also be the nucleus of any future ministerial group. But, more than that, they were the most articulate and persuasive representatives of that bureaucratic, centralised and reformed France governed by a monarchy with genuine executive powers and an Assembly representing property, however acquired, which touched the aristocratic emigration on a raw nerve. It was unforgivable.

As increasing numbers of the early membership of the Constituent Assembly found their way into emigration the debate spread through the European capitals, especially London, and lost none of its intensity; and even though the bureaucratic and administrative element in the *monarchien* case diminished what remained was no less unacceptable to the 'pures'. It amounted to the concept of a written constitution, the need to accept the fact of the Revolution, its popular appeal and the necessity of working within its framework. Calonne was to put himself finally outside the pale of princely and aristocratic recognition by making just such a demand for realism in 1796. In the previous year he had already urged a written constitution. Now he asked 'Do we want to go on applying the old principles, the old methods, the old assumptions to an entirely new order of things? What is the use of precedents in a situation without precedents?' And he went on to deny the existence of an old constitution. The existence of such a constitution was an article of faith among the 'pures'. Almost the whole of their case rested upon it.

Other *monarchien* politicians and publicists went on pressing the argument for realism. Mallet du Pan, a Swiss journalist and friend of Malouet and Montlosier, more clearly a *monarchien* than Calonne, argued persistently in 1793 for adaptation to the new demands of the Revolution and an understanding of its popular base. By 1795, although a critic originally of the 1791 constitution, he was arguing its merits and the impossibility of a return to 1789. Montlosier (whose views Calonne had largely been repeating in 1796) also stressed the need to recognise the force of the Revolution rather than go on applying the same inflexible code. The 'pures' remained resolutely opposed to any such heresy. 'I would rather see France perish than reduced to that level of ignominy', said d'Antraigues. There was, in short, no room for compromise, no understanding, in a battle which raged through English and continental émigré circles and which stirred up not just revolutionary conflicts but a basic division of *ancien régime* government and society over the nature of the monarchy. It was through this maze that the British government and its agents found themselves wandering as they turned in 1794 to consider a restoration of the monarchy as the means to their objectives.

In the autumn of 1794 the British government had been attracted by a plan of Mallet's for a restoration of the monarchy through the union of constitutional monarchists and moderates in the Convention. The Foreign Secretary, Grenville, sent William Wickham to Switzerland to investigate the possibilities but the whole scheme collapsed because there was no basis in the Convention for it, or any monarchical unity. Wickham, who stayed on in Berne as chargé d'affaires, turned to other schemes for subverting the Republic by internal revolt aided by invasion. The outbreak of the Vendéan revolt in March 1793 made the West the main focal point of popular royalism and the most promising area in which to establish the base from which a restoration might take place, although it was never to the exclusion of older areas of insurrection in the South, or the appeal of Lyons. Indeed, the South exercised a stronger pull on large numbers of émigrés than the West ever did. They may have understood it more.

The problem with providing assistance for internal revolt remained the same as it had been from the beginning of the popular disturbances against the Revolution when Coblenz had tried to respond to the appeals of Froment and the Allier brothers. What was really going on? Information was almost always sketchy, inaccurate and out-of-date. The level of assistance reflected these problems. For example, in November 1793 the British sent an expedition under Lord Moira to supply the rebel attack on the Normandy port of Granville but it arrived too late and in December the Vendéans were decisively defeated as an organised force. Because the western insurrection now broke up into irregular bands, or *chouans*, information was even more difficult to obtain. A few supplies were sent from England in 1794 but only one, quite inadequate, shipload reached the West.

The British government nevertheless prepared a major initiative for 1795 based on the strategy of internal insurrection linked with invasion by a mixed allied and émigré army. It had been sufficiently impressed by the optimistic claims made by the commander of the upper Breton *chouans*, the comte de Puisaye, as to the forces at his disposal, to plan an émigré landing from a British fleet in Brittany. It would be tied in with risings in eastern and south-eastern France and an invasion by the Austrians and Condé's reinvigorated army. The landing took place in June 1795 close to the Quiberon peninsula in Brittany. It was a disastrous failure, a record of misunderstanding and dispute, particularly between the two émigré commanders, Puisaye and d'Hervilly. In mid-July those who were unable to get away surrendered to the Republican forces under General Hoche. Nearly 750 were shot.

In spite of this fiasco Pitt could convince himself that not all was lost. Prussia, Holland and Spain had withdrawn from the war even before Quiberon, but there remained the other part of the strategy: the risings in the east, fomented by Wickham, the possibility of buying the French commander on the Rhine, Pichegru, and a successful offensive by the Austrians, with Condé, on which Wickham had spent £15,000. This too collapsed in unrelieved disaster, even if not costly in lives as Quiberon had been. The failure of a rising by conservative Sections in Paris on 5 October (13 Vendémiaire) persuaded Pichegru that the time was not right to sell out to the royalists. Consequently he defeated the projected invasion by the Austrians and their commander, Clerfayt, thereupon ceased campaigning for the rest of the year. Condé's army had not been used. The planned rising in the Franche-Comté and the Lyonnais failed to materialise, in part because the republican authorities were aware of them and able to take preventive action.

A final ember remained of the whole grand scheme. In the west the British had planned, after Quiberon, to land a force on the island of Noirmoutier close to the Vendéan coast from where contact could be made with the main rebel commander in the area, Charette. The landing was not, however, possible and instead it was diverted to the Ile d'Yeu considerably further out from the coast, on 30 September. Artois joined it the next day. There he remained, in spite of the pleas of Charette to join him, and although much was to be made of Artois' apparent cowardice, and of his expressed contempt for irregular warfare, his decision made sense: there was confusion over a meeting place and Charette's latest campaign was going badly. Artois sent him a sword and words of encouragement instead of his presence, much to Charette's scorn. The émigrés stayed on the Ile d'Yeu through worsening weather and supplies until at the end of November they were evacuated. Artois returned to Portsmouth, where he was not allowed to land because of the danger of arrest for debt. He went instead to Holyrood House in Edinburgh where he remained for the next three years.

British policy, then, ended 1795 in disarray: three different courses of action had been followed and all had failed. The attack on the

French West Indies had yielded territory but had not squeezed the French hard enough economically to bring the war to an end, while at the same time it had confirmed the suspicions, which alone united all brands of monarchist, that Britain was interested primarily in commercial gain. It had also helped to distance Britain from its Coalition allies and restricted its room for diplomatic manoeuvre by making it difficult for any agreement with France which might involve the abandonment of these gains. The advance from the north through Flanders had fallen apart. And finally the schemes to encourage internal insurrection had come to nothing. Considerable sums of money had apparently been spent to no advantage.

Wickham, who had been responsible for disbursing so much of that money, was still in Switzerland as the main British agent in contact with counter-revolutionary groups. By the end of 1795 he had learnt some realism and a more accurate assessment of the personalities and situation but he still had to weave his way through the complexities of émigré politics, between the popular royalism of 'interior' France, which he barely understood, and the unrealistic aims of 'exterior' France. There remained also the conservative elements of property-owning moderate republicans which might be won over to a monarchy by an acceptable programme – the policy, in fact, which Wickham had been sent to Switzerland the year before in order to investigate. At the beginning of 1796 he was still attracted to the idea of insurrection in the south but in the spring, faced with the Austrian refusal to move and the French successes in Italy, that idea had to be abandoned. There remained the constitutional methods tentatively explored in 1794. The opportunity to develop this policy would present itself with the elections to the French Assembly due in 1797. It was hoped that the remaining elements of the old Convention could then be entirely or largely replaced by moderate republicans or royalists. It was a very attractive policy but fraught with problems: there was the difficulty of securing reliable information on the politics of the Directory; the considerable suspicions in émigré circles of British intentions and good faith; the divisions even amongst the 'pures' themselves; and the enormous gulf between the constitutionals and the 'pures' which would have to be bridged if that stable, generally acceptable, moderate constitutional monarchy which the British wanted were to be established in France.

Information was the weak point. There was no lack of quantity but accuracy was quite another matter. Combined with poor security, unreliable allies and a strong dash of the perpetual wishful thinking of émigré circles disaster was never far off. The most important source of information available to the émigré princes was the spy network known as the Paris Agency which since 1791 had been feeding material to d'Antraigues for onward transmission. The members of the Agency were people with much the same prejudices as d'Antraigues, including a preference for Spain over Austria as the main source of potential help. D'Antraigues supplemented their information from other sources such as Imbert and Froment, and added his own interpretation. Much of it was therefore fiction from start to finish. Mallet du Pan called the Agency 'inept, indiscreet . . . imprudent, and totally lacking in judgement'. Part at least of the confusion among the *chouans* during the Quiberon expedition may have been due to its deliberate spreading of misinformation.

In spite of all this, the Agency was in a key situation at the turn of 1795–6. Its own position was starting to coincide with Wickham's as he moved from support for subversion and insurrection to more constitutional methods. The impetus for their change of front, like Wickham's, came from the failure of the alternatives: the withdrawal of Spain from the war in July 1795, and the collapse of the Vendéan insurrection. In addition there were rumours that a different candidate for the throne, perhaps an Orléanist, might be found. The Agency was in a pivotal position by the end of 1795: it was now sending information direct to Provence (or Louis XVIII as he had been called since June) and it was also the link between the West, now the responsibility of Artois, and the East, supervised by Précy.

From the British point of view a major weakness of the Agency was its failure to renounce force even if it might be concealed by a mask of constitutionality which took the form of a system of electoral agents covering a secret organisation ready to strike at Paris if need be. That was the sort of thing which alarmed moderates, whether monarchist or republican. It was essential to show that a restoration meant peace, order and reconciliation. A starting point would be the declaration of an amnesty by the Pretender, 'Louis XVIII', accompanied by a realistic programme. That was the central problem.

We have seen that the basis of the alliance between the princes and the provincial aristocracy who formed the bulk of their following in the emigration was the Declaration of 23 June 1789. It was restated in the Declaration of Hamm issued by Louis XVIII in January 1793 on the news of the execution of his brother. The monarchy would be reestablished on the 'unalterable bases of its Constitution and the reformation of abuses' together with the restoration of property and the punishment of the guilty. Although the manifesto did not meet with the approval of everyone in the circle around Provence (as he then was), for émigrés of like mind it was exactly what they wanted to hear, the re-echoing of that hard line 'no surrender' which had been heard from the princes since the beginning of the emigration. A further Declaration was issued, from Verona, on the news of the death of the young Louis XVII in June 1795. Again it made no substantial change other than to offer an amnesty to all except regicides and making no mention of the *parlements* or of confiscating land. Louis XVIII may have considered it moderate but Mallet du Pan saw no hope in an 'amnesty which merely offered not to hang them' and it was in reality a rejection of the moderates. D'Antraigues had helped in its drafting. The Pretender and his circle showed no signs of developing understanding or realism. 'The old constitution of France', he told Lord Macartney, who had been sent to persuade him to adopt a more flexible attitude and also issue an amnesty, 'was the wisdom of the ages, the perfection of reason', although he intended 'to remove the rust with which time clothes all the best human institutions'. That was in August 1795. A year later, in September, Wickham was still despairing of shifting attitudes: 'It is indeed but too evident, that all views of humanity, of policy, of Justice, even of Interest are but light in the scale when opposed to the desire of humbling and punishing the first authors of the Revolution.' Shifting their views was going to be an uphill task.

Although he was never to succeed in moving Louis XVIII more than a fraction, he went ahead with the plan for a restoration by constitutional means because the conditions inside France for such a restoration were looking increasingly promising. It was nevertheless a delicate business involving bringing together groups who normally at best distrusted, and at worst loathed, each other. The task of promoting that 'union of parties' on which the whole thing depended very largely fell to a former representative of the Provençal nobility in the Estates General and member of the Constituent Assembly, Antoine-Joseph d'André. In effect, at the beginning of 1796 he became a salaried employee of the British government working through Wickham. D'André was a far more reliable and astute individual than the members of the Paris Agency, with more contacts and a sounder grasp of electoral politics. He was in touch with a wide circle of constitutional royalists and moderate republicans, especially a group known as the 'Clichy Club'.

Wickham also gave £10,000 to an electoral organisation known as the Philanthrophic Institutes which, as their name indicates, masqueraded as charitable associations. They were of questionable value – in fact probably a liability rather than an advantage to the cause of moderate royalism. That was for a very important reason. It was vital that there should be no suggestion of the use of force to secure a restoration. It was just such an element in the Paris Agency which the Directory was able to exploit early in 1797 when it was betrayed and largely broken up. Many of the members of the Institutes also had a background of support for violence, hardly surprisingly since the germ of the whole idea had been bred by the Agency. The head of the Toulouse branch until the end of 1797, Pourquery du Bourg, had been involved in royalist terror for some years, while the lower levels of membership both here and at Bordeaux were specialists in the street brawl. A pattern common to these Institutes was an outwardly respectable organisation masking an inner group, known as *Côterie des Fils Légitimes* or in some cases by a similar title, whose task was the preparation of insurrection.

The anxieties such people could produce among constitutional royalists points up the fundamental weakness of the whole policy pursued by Wickham and the British government in 1794–7, and less enthusiastically down to 1799. Most of those identified as 'royalists' were nothing of the sort. They were moderate republicans interested in orderly and stable government based on the rights of property. The intransigence of the 'pures' and their association with violence easily frightened them. Wickham's jubilation at the results of the elections of March 1797, when almost all the former Conventionnels failed to be returned, was therefore misplaced, as d'André warned him.

A key element was still missing: a clear change of direction in the policies of Louis XVIII. Even a slight shift in March 1797, in a Declaration from his latest refuge at Blankenburg, was enough to shock his supporters. It promised no vengeance even against regicides, a willingness to listen to public opinion, and more stress on the reform of the 'old constitution'. There was still no denunciation of force. It was an omission underlined by his efforts to revive the old Paris Agency under the name of 'Council' and by his reluctance to work fully with Wickham and d'André. He needed British money but at the same time tried to circumvent its conditions and follow his own schemes such as a plan to smuggle the duc de Berry, his nephew, into Paris at an appropriate time.

The whole foundation of the plan for a constitutional restoration was therefore insecure. It was anyway well known to the Directors after the capture of d'Antraigues in Trieste in June together with a large collection of incriminating documents which Bonaparte forwarded, suitably edited to remove his name, to the government. The revelation of Pichegru's involvement (he had been elected President of the Five Hundred in March) and of the vast sums spent by Wickham on buying up the deputies, was enough to bring together the triumvirate of Reubell, La Révellière and Barras in defence of the Republic. A show of strength by the triumvirate in July, which included bringing detachments from the army of the newly appointed Minister of War, Hoche, to Paris, foreshadowed the coup against the Right on 18 Fructidor (4 September). It fell with overwhelming force on a leaderless, confused and hesitant Right, already divided and demoralised. Most of them anyway preferred an acceptable Republic to a monarchy which had scarcely budged an inch from Hamm and Verona. The enormous gulf between constitutional royalism and the 'pures' can be seen in the comment of Mallet du Pan that 'it is as impossible to recreate the *ancien régime* as it is to build Saint Peter's in Rome with chimney dust', 'The great majority of the French will never willingly give in to the former authority and those who wielded it', he had written to Louis XVIII after the Declaration of Verona.

There was never again to be an opportunity for a peaceful restoration such as there had been in 1797. Subsequent plans all involved insurrection and invasion although British policy always insisted on evidence of internal support and a base within France from which restoration could be carried out. As for the émigré princes, although there were to be significant shifts in approach, most of the old problems dogged them: wayward allied support, the insecurity of their plans, the divisions among their own following, and perhaps most important, their inability to escape being identified with disorder and even civil war. Fresh networks of agents were put together after the disaster of 1797. The most important of these was the Swabian Agency established at Ulm in March 1798 and including d'André and Précy among its members. It was linked with Louis XVIII's Secret Royal Council in Paris, a group of agents under Royer-Collard. The purpose of this Council was something more than just the gathering of information to be passed on to the Swabian Agency: it also had the more ambitious task of acting as the 'shadow' government, in the event of a restoration, before the arrival of the king.

In 1798 this new structure was at the heart of a fresh plan concocted by Wickham, together with the reconstituted Philanthropic Institutes, for a co-ordinated series of risings linked to invasion. Insurrections would take place in the West, the South and the South-west timed to coincide with an invasion by the Second Coalition from Switzerland and an Anglo-Russian landing in Holland. It was important that the risings should be simultaneous. That was never a possibility: rivalries in the South-west between Bordeaux and Toulouse, in the persons of their respective leaders, Dupont-Constant and Pourquery, made co-operation difficult. The result was that the risings were scattered through August and September and easily picked off by the Republicans, with heavy losses to the royalists in the Toulouse region. There were early successes in the West, with the capture by the royalists of Le Mans and Nantes, but the great days of western Counter-Revolution had passed and their victories were brief. This in itself is an indication that the peasantry were not simply the passive instruments of aristocratic leaders. By the end of the year the region had been largely pacified. The Coalition's early successes had also run their course by the end of the year. Bonaparte's victory at Marengo over the Austrians in 1800 set the seal on the allied failure and on plans for yet another attempt at rebellion in the South linked to foreign and émigré invasion. That was the end, in comprehensive defeat, of a policy stretching back to the beginnings of the emigration.

The organisations which had sustained the policy now steadily fell apart and their personnel scattered. 18 Brumaire was widely welcomed by all those whose sole interest in a restoration had been stability and security against the possibility of a return to Jacobin Terror. The Philanthropic Institutes disintegrated retaining, it has been suggested, just a shadowy framework of irreconcilables who came back into the open when the Napoleonic system collapsed in 1814. It had been hoped that Bonaparte would prove to be a restorer of the monarchy and in February 1800 Louis XVIII had urged him to do so. Bonaparte's reply in September ('you must not hope for your return to France; you would have to walk over a hundred thousand corpses . . .') closed the door on any chance of a negotiated restoration. The Swabian Agency, already creaking under internal strains, was broken up in 1801 through a mixture of Fouché's spies and the advance of French troops into southern Germany. The Secret Royal Council seems to have survived as late as 1804 although Royer-Collard's correspondence with Louis XVIII had already stopped. In addition to all the problems of organisation and support, the members of these various bodies were nearly all on bad terms with each other. In the case of Royer-Collard there is also an early indication of the emergence of a new breed of royalist who would be more at home in the July Monarchy than in the Revolution: a monarchist of reason rather than sentiment, looking towards a reformed monarchy above party, symbolising national unity and the *juste milieu*. It was a little too early for that.

Artois had his own network which followed a somewhat different course. His Agency – the 'English Agency', so-called after its pay-masters – was broken up by Fouché in 1800 but conspiracies linked to Artois continued to flourish although they were not directly the responsibility of Artois himself. Rather they were the work of a diminishing band of émigrés and surviving *chouans*. They were diminishing because an increasing number took advantage of successive changes in the law which allowed them to return to France. The émigré lists had been closed in March 1800; and in 1802 an amnesty was extended to all except those who continued to bear arms. The Concordat of 1800 encouraged the return of large numbers of priests. The mass held on Easter Day 1802 to celebrate the conclusion of the Concordat also, suggests Doyle, seemed a celebration of 'the burial of the Revolution'. Only the hard core of émigré survivors were thus left in exile, other than those who chose to settle permanently abroad. The old policies of conspiracy and invasion were therefore even more fanciful, and now irrelevant, than ever.

There were two ambitious plots. The first in 1800 was a plan to blow Bonaparte up on 24 December in rue Saint-Nicaise in Paris. There was considerable loss of life and Fouché, a pioneer in modern secret police methods, used it to round up surviving Jacobins who had in no way been involved. Artois almost certainly knew about the plot, just as he did of the second one in 1804. Cadoudal, the Breton *chouan* leader, was a central figure in this as he had been in rue Saint-Nicaise. Pichegru was to attempt to neutralise the army by suborning another general as a prelude to the kidnapping of Bonaparte when a prince of the House of Bourbon arrived, probably Artois. It would all coincide with a rising in the Rhineland paid for by the British agent in the region. The whole plot was uncovered and the leading figures arrested. Cadoudal was executed, Pichegru found dead in his cell, perhaps by suicide. The most spectacular consequence of it all was the abduction in Baden of Condé's son, the duc d'Enghien, his summary trial and execution. It was meant as an example to all future conspirators of the ruthless exercise of power in defence of the regime. It was something that scarcely needed demonstrating.

Louis XVIII had never approved of the type of conspiracy represented by rue Saint-Nicaise and the Cadoudal Plot. 'A cowardly atrocity', his private secretary called the latter. In the end, however, plots and invasions and all the other plans came to an end because the means were no longer available. There was nothing further to be done except wait on events and that meant the military defeat of the Emperor by the allies. The only hope there was that the British, after the failure of the short peace in 1802, were more committed to that policy than ever before.

There was some movement in the painful progress towards accepting the reality of the situation. This was done in the usual way, that is under the cover of a smokescreen pretending that the princes' policy had not changed. A memorandum in 1799 praised the Verona Declaration but accepted the impossibility of restoring everything as it had been in 1789 and the need to retain the existing judicial and administrative structure. In 1800 another Declaration went further and promised a total amnesty. In 1804 Louis and Artois met, in Sweden, for the first time in eleven years and, while reasserting Bourbon claims, finally buried the Declaration of Verona. There was to be a total amnesty and the retention of the administrative and judicial structure, the maintenance of officials in their posts, the confirmation of the ranks of army officers, the defence of private and public liberties. Only over the Church lands was there some hesitation, where they would adopt 'an attitude in accordance with the wishes of the nation'. The Declaration of Kalmar, as it was called, was deliberately dated 2 December 1804, the day of Bonaparte's coronation. It could scarcely have made more concessions and even those were, when the restoration did occur, to prove a bitter pill for a great many émigrés and leaders of popular royalism to swallow.

It made no difference in 1804. It was ignored by everybody, including all the European powers to whom Louis sent a protest at the casting aside of the rights of legitimacy. The Bourbons were spectators of events over which they had no influence. In 1807 the Tsar met Louis XVIII, 'I have just met the most ineffectual and insignificant man in Europe', he wrote. 'He will never ascend the throne'. In the same year Louis arrived in England and, two years later, set up his little Court at Hartwell near Aylesbury. Here he led the life of an English country gentleman, for which he had little taste, and in a climate which he loathed. That, and his gout which, with a growing corpulence, in the end virtually immobilised him, made life miserable. Artois had his own diminishing band of associates in the neighbourhood of Baker Street, the favoured district of the better-off end of the emigration. The dying exhortations of his mistress in 1804 led him to a more pious life. As for political activity, all they could do was wait on events.

4

The Defeat of the Interior Counter-Revolution

Both the émigré leadership and the revolutionary governments made assumptions about popular royalism which clouded their judgement either in trying to suppress it or take advantage of it. Both made the same error in failing to recognise its genuine popular roots. It was an autonomous movement, with its own leadership, its own aspirations and grievances. Revolutionary governments readily fell back on a conspiracy theory, or a peasantry corrupted by superstition, priesthood and aristocracy. This seemed the only explanation of such blindness to the benefits of Revolution. The answer to this, as it appeared to the often desperate authorities, was the wholesale slaughter or removal of the population, just as Fréron and Barras had advised in 1793 in the case of the people of Marseilles, an equally inexplicable and intractable problem. The lessons had to be painfully learned before the right combination of military force and political concession brought the risings in the West to an end. The Midi was to remain, even more than the West, a focal point of active popular royalism well into the restoration period although, since Counter-Revolution did not become an expression of its cultural identity and it was a more divided region, it was not marked to the same enduring extent by the revolutionary upheavals. The émigré aristocracy and the princes, on the other hand, misunderstood the limitations to popular royalism. It was never the blind devotion, or simple loyalty, of a faithful people but rather a declaration of opposition to a Revolution which had failed to deliver its promises and had also attacked the traditional relationships and communal forms of the insurrectionary regions. A number of émigrés who arrived to lend their services to the rebels in the West soon found themselves at cross-purposes and frequently left in disgust. The gap in comprehension between the two main streams of the Counter-

Revolution was to be a central weakness of the whole opposition to the revolutionary tradition. Through the nineteenth century Legitimists, the heirs to Counter-Revolution, were to fail to develop a sound popular base because they both mistrusted it and misinterpreted it. The roots of that can be seen in the revolutionary period itself.

The risings in the West occurred with a speed which took the authorities by surprise even though much of the region, as we saw in Chapter 2, had been seriously disturbed for about two years. Nevertheless, north of the Loire where towns were larger and communications better the National Guards were able to intervene swiftly and energetically in support of rural patriots and the risings broke up into isolated bands of insurgents known as *chouans*. South of the Loire the situation was different. Here, in the 'Vendée' troops and National Guards were thinly spread, towns few, and authority remote. This was always the key to the success or failure of counter-revolutionary insurrection whether in France itself or in French-occupied territories. The Vendée developed as it did because in the first weeks the rebels were allowed to win some startling successes in overwhelming the small towns of the region, although they were never strong enough to hold them for long. The outlines of armies and leadership also emerged rapidly although this also need not be taken too seriously, for all its apparent sophistication.

The first leaders of the Vendéan revolt came from the peasant world: the most famous, a folk-hero in the making, was a pedlar, Cathelineau; another, who survived longer, was a gamekeeper, Stofflet. Among Breton *chouannerie*, as compared to the Vendéan variety, this plebeian leadership was to remain fairly prominent, at least until 1795. Cadoudal's popular origins were part of his appeal, although he was by no means poor. Even so, the nobility early on assumed a prominent role and provided most of the leadership above the level of the small district bands. The Vendéan rebels sought them out in the first few days. This was not through affection – the nobility provided military expertise and perhaps access to arms. There was also a long tradition in peasant revolt of expecting the aristocracy to provide a lead whether they wanted to or not. In the Vendée some clearly did not, or were at least very reluctant. However, they were expected, as principal inhabitants of the community, to live up to certain responsibilities and codes of conduct: the original concept of the role of seigneur had not entirely died. It was a role generally accepted by the local aristocracy.

The peasantry they led was never straightforwardly submissive or deferential. The leadership always had to take into account the spontaneously popular origins of a revolt which showed little or no interest in the larger issues and command structure of the Counter-Revolution. Loyalty was to a particular leader who was expected to provide certain qualities of courage and command. They had to lead from the front: the casualty rate among the rebel commanders is perhaps an indication of this. Each commander developed his own style, reflecting not just differences of character but the varied backgrounds from which the aristocracy came. Their personal followings were jealously guarded and any infringements on their command bitterly resisted. In April 1794, for example, one of the leaders, Marigny, resentful at being excluded from an agreement, refused to join an operation and was executed on the orders of Stofflet and another leader, Charette. As a result his band removed itself from the orders of the other commanders. Charette never got on particularly well with any of the other commanders, especially Stofflet, who resented the noble leaders and the émigrés. Disputes with 'subordinate' leaders, as the Marigny case shows, were settled briskly: Charette had one 'general', Launay, murdered. The peasantry obeyed only the orders which suited them, could never be relied upon to turn up in sufficient numbers for an action unless there was some chance of success, and melted away afterwards. This was usually once the looting and drinking which followed any success was over. Weaponry was always in short supply and consisted of whatever could be captured or came to hand, such as farm implements. The stately and formalised courtesies of eighteenth-century warfare, apart from rare and much vaunted exceptions such as Bonchamp's pardon of the republican prisoners just before his own death, were ignored. Prisoners were routinely slaughtered, and the bodies often mutilated. No wonder many of the émigré aristocrats arriving to join the rebellion were bewildered and horrified by what they found.

In part this was also because the information seeping through to the outside world was scanty and inaccurate. That information, fed by optimistic and interested individuals, could easily mislead the emigration and the allies into thinking that they were dealing with properly organised and disciplined armies with a formal command structure. Nothing could be further from the truth. The theoretical organisation of the rebel 'armies' was impressive but in practice meant little. The 'Catholic and Royal Army' which made its appearance south of the

Loire in April was only one of a number of groupings. The *Conseil Supérieur* set up to administer conquered territories had little effective authority, while the *Conseil Militaire*, supposedly responsible for strategy, could rarely count, without enormous difficulty, on the obedience of all the commanders. The various commanders-in-chief similarly had limited authority over a collection of temperamental individualists. The recruitment of the armies through parish committees which summoned the peasantry by the sounding of the tocsin or arranging the sails of windmills in a particular way, worked only haphazardly.

It was the feebleness of the opposition which allowed the rebels to carry all before them during the summer of 1793. However, the effectiveness of the methods used by the Vendéans cannot be ignored. These were the techniques of irregular warfare, perfectly adapted to the terrain and to their forces: the surprise attack, the ambush, concentration at the enemy's weak point, retreat through the labrynthine countryside if the enemy resisted or arrived in strength. Such tactics were not new: they were a feature of every peasant revolt and have become familiar since. However, it was nearly a century since French armies had had to face such a problem and the means of dealing with it had to be relearned, the troops assembled in the right numbers and at the right place, and with the training and discipline to carry out the methods of counter-insurgency, as we would now call it. That meant, also, that military methods had to be accompanied locally and centrally by the political sensitivity needed to tackle the roots of the insurrection.

A dominating military present was essential to the re-establishment of government authority but a purely military solution, once the revolt had passed its initial stages, was never successful. That was not for want of determination. Many of the republican commanders in the West may have been incompetent in the early stages, the troops inexperienced, poorly supplied, the command divided. By the end of the summer in 1793 that situation was improving. In August the Convention decreed the total destruction of the Vendée and sent Kléber with 12,000 seasoned troops to the West with virtually complete command over operations there. By the end of the year the remnants of the Vendéan army had been destroyed and most of the leading figures of the great revolt were dead. Kléber's military methods of dealing with *chouannerie* were also, in the end, to be successful: small detachments of men scattered through the insurrectionary zone to defend the patriots and engage in 'search and destroy' operations against the guerrillas.

The government, however, was in no mood for anything but the sharpest of lessons: a new commander, Turreau, appointed to the Army of the West in November 1793, adopted a completely different approach from the one outlined by Kléber. It was a purely military solution which was to contribute, probably more effectively than the revolt itself, to marking out the Vendée as a distinctive political region of France with a sense of identity derived from the experience of its treatment. Turreau's aim was to isolate the region, destroy its resources, and move the loyal population to other areas. Mobile columns, soon to be called *colonnes infernales*, criss-crossed the Vendée destroying farms and crops, carrying out summary executions and treating the whole insurrectionary zone as it might a conquered foreign country. The policy failed, although the Vendéan rebels were still unable to co-operate. The Republicans ran out of supplies in a devastated countryside, discipline broke down, patriots found themselves being treated as if they also were rebels, and a whole population was being alienated, making ultimate conciliation even more remote. Turreau's policy was abandoned and Kléber's restored. This was put in the hands, eventually, of the last and the ablest of the Republican generals in the West, Lazare Hoche.

Hoche was able to combine military skill with strong Republican loyalties, a political awareness and an understanding of a range of opinion, perhaps sharpened by a spell in the Conciergerie prison between April and July 1794. In August he was appointed to command the *armée des côtes de Cherbourg* with Canclaux commanding, from October, in the Vendée itself. A new representative, Boursault, more sympathetic to a fresh approach, was sent to the armies of Brest and Cherbourg, which in November were unified under Hoche's single command. He still did not have things all his own way – the Convention for example was sometimes uneasy over his policy of religious toleration – but he was able to implement the mix of military firmness and political moderation which in the end succeeded. Hoche accepted the need to recognise certain realities in the region, above all the peasant wish for religious freedom. In addition, he considered that the peasantry was not very interested in politics, or even very royalist. 'It only knows its priests and its cattle', he said on one occasion. The answer therefore was to guarantee the place of the former and return the latter against assurances of good behaviour. Garrisons placed throughout the countryside sent out constant patrols, day and night, of well-disciplined troops, using paths rather than roads, to check the small bands of *chouans*, search out arms, and protect the 'sound' citizen from the rebel. Supporters of the rebels were ruthlessly punished, usually by the confiscation of grain and cattle. On the other hand, refractory priests were persuaded to come out of hiding, informers were encouraged, the peaceable protected. Religious feelings were respected, old place-names restored even when they included a saint's name. Military pragmatism was the order of the day rather than political dogma. 'I aspire less to the fame of a conqueror than to the role of peace-maker', said Hoche. 'Do we need to shoot people to enlighten them?' he was to ask the Directory in March 1796.

It was a policy which began to pay considerable dividends. By the beginning of 1795 most of the rebel bands were in a desperate situation. Charette signed an armistice on generous terms in January and other leaders followed. He had no intention of keeping it, he informed London. It was a superficial lull in the rebellion, meant to buy time: many of the rebel leaders had been unhappy with the agreements, as had Hoche, and they soon broke down. The renewed insurrection was, however, quite unable to match its old ferocity. There was little possibility of Charette, for example, being able to assist the landings at Quiberon in June. The place of the Quiberon landings in the wider strategy of the British government and émigré politics was dealt with in the last chapter. It was not as foolhardy as might at first appear. The place was chosen according to information which suggested that the most active of the *chouan* bands, particularly Cadoudal's, would be able to give their support, and that Charette could reach the area. Most of this was misleading, having come from the ever-optimistic Breton commander Puisaye, and in addition the various rebel bands had been constantly harried by the Republicans. Quiberon was a devastating defeat: 6000 prisoners fell into Republican hands. The execution of 748 of them, on the orders of the local representative on mission, was intended in part as a warning to other émigrés of the consequences of such adventures.

Further efforts to link the western risings with external support during the rest of 1795 were also a failure. Artois' landing on the Ile d'Yeu to hold himself in readiness for a fresh insurrection in the Vendée came to nothing. Charette was in no position to safeguard a landing on the coast and Artois' unwillingness to risk it was sensible even if the whole episode was to be used as evidence of some contempt for the *chouans* and possibly his own cowardice.

At the end of the year the steady accumulation of authority under

Hoche was completed when he was given command over all the armies of the West – the *armée des côtes de l'Océan* – and primacy over the civil power, virtually dictatorial powers in nearly twenty Departments, an extraordinary elevation for a young general only twenty-seven years old. In spite of differences with the local administrations, in the end he was able to count on the support of the central government and enjoy a freedom from political interference denied to his predecessors. The rebel bands were pursued, their leaders captured. Stofflet was executed in February, Charette in March, others were persuaded to submit and leave the country. In July the western rebellion was at an end.

Many problems remained to provide the fuel for further outbreaks but these were only a pale and half-hearted reflection of 1793–6. The West remained unsettled as long as the government was unable to pursue a consistent line of religious toleration; while garrisons made their exactions on the surrounding population; and the sporadic violence of ex-*chouans* kept alive a sense of insecurity. That formed the background to a fresh rising in 1798–9, although it was also a part of one of the ambitious schemes put together by the princes for internal risings linked to foreign invasion. In the West the comte de Bourmont set about trying to restore the shattered fabric of *chouannerie* and give it the military organisation it had lacked. The aim was to launch an attack on the poorly defended towns of the West and from that base roll on to a reconquest of France for the monarchy. It was a difficult year for the authorities almost everywhere in France and outside it too – 1798–9 saw the most serous uprisings against French rule in the conquered territories of Europe. Large areas of the Midi, particularly Provence, were in the hands of brigands claiming royalist allegiances. However, the whole scheme was unco-ordinated and the successes in the West, although spectacular in that they included the capture of Le Mans and Nantes, were short-lived. The risings in the South-west with which it was supposed to have been co-ordinated had already been defeated with heavy loss in August. By the end of November Bourmont had succumbed to the pressure from government forces and his dwindling support. An armistice brought the rising to an end.

Bonaparte used a combination of ruthlessness and concession to complete the subjugation of the West. The Norman *chouan* leader Frotté, for example, was shot while being taken to Paris under safe conduct; on the other hand exemption from conscription and the settlement of the religious question met some of the region's strongest grievances. The Napoleonic Prefect of the Department of the Vendée was a royalist, the baron de Barante, who helped Mme de la Rochejacquelein, widow of the prominent rebel leader, to write her memoirs. The process of pacification was also helped by war-weariness and the prospect for the leaders, like Bourmont, of careers in the new regime. Bonaparte also gave his attention to one of the gaps which had allowed the insurrection to assume such enormous proportions in the first place. The communications were improved and a garrison town built at La Roche-sur-Yon. There were to be two further risings in the West in 1815 and 1832 but neither was on any great scale. They were notable for the feebleness of their popular support. That in itself is another indication of the nature of these insurrections: they were above all a response to deeply felt grievances which expressed itself in traditional form under traditional leadership. Their royalism was less a profession of devotion to the monarchy than a declaration of opposition to a Revolution which had deluded the opinion-makers among the rural population with false promises and accompanied this with an assault on its values and way of life. They were revolts which were local in origins and objectives. The noble leadership struggled in vain to give them a wider national purpose.

The insurrection and its suppression cost the insurrectionary zone perhaps a quarter of its population and in the case of some communes nearly a half. The population of Cholet, the economic centre of the Mauges, fell from just under 8500 in 1790 to about 2000 in 1797. Possibly about 250,000 people were killed, not counting the losses on the republican side. These, and the atrocities of which they were a part, formed the experiences which helped in the process of giving the rural West a badge of identity. The Vendée, simply a department in 1792, emerged as a distinctive region. It was to remain for a century or more the bastion of royalist conservatism but this was more an evocation of its past, a statement of its distinction, than a sign of deep loyalty to social superiors. The Church and nobility liked, through carnivals and so on, to keep the memories alive and use them perhaps to sustain a proper social hierarchy. Radicals were, it is true, always to be outsiders in the rural West but that did not mean that the aristocracy had the special link with the people which they liked to believe. As always there was something of an element of mutual convenience and a dash of make-believe in it all. In 1814, as the Napoleonic regime disintegrated, it was in the South-west and the South that the main indications of some support for the Bourbons came although even much of that had to be manufactured.

The new regime had a more difficult task in pacifying the South. The whole region south of Lyons had remained disturbed almost continuously since 1789. White Terror in 1795 merged into other forms of carefully directed violence against old enemies, personal, social or political – often all three. These were by no means random attacks. The plans for a large-scale insurrection supported by invasion in 1798–9 had given a special place to the South, just as the schemes for a restoration by electoral means had in 1796–7. The South had always been favoured by many émigrés as a more fruitful area for establishing a base than the West. The leaders of popular royalism such as Froment or Dominique Allier kept close links with the emigration, particularly with Précy in Switzerland, and their influence spread far beyond their native areas. Lyons provided a convenient and sympathetic meeting point, something like a headquarters of southern Counter-Revolution. The apparently 'mindless' acts of savage vengeance against former agents and sympathisers of the Terror by 'Companies of the Sun' or 'Companies of Jesus' after Thermidor, in 1795, were therefore organised and directed by people like Allier and others who had cause to resent the exactions and confiscations of the Revolution.

In that they had the support of the vast numbers of poor and all those in rural and urban society whose traditional ways of life and sources of income, for example, in common rights to pasture and waste, had been destroyed by the Revolution to the benefit of the bourgeoisie. The central thread of popular Counter-Revolution, whether in the West or the South, is again clear: the resistance of communities to the centralising, individualistic threat posed by the Revolution to traditional patterns of life. That resistance took traditional forms in all areas, peasant revolt, communal isolation of 'outsiders' or *intrus*, even the use, for this purpose, of the snake-like group dance known as the *farandole*. It was not, therefore, a pointless brigandage, in spite of appearances, either in composition or motivation or aims, but carefully directed towards undermining the administration of the region and reducing confidence in the regular authorities – 'destabilisation' as it might now be called. Moreover, in 1796–7 it had the wider aim of securing a royalist electoral victory. That came very close to success, as we have seen, only to be frustrated by the *coup* of Fructidor. Counter-revolutionary brigandage took on after that a wider, rural, character which still succeeded in making much of the Midi ungovernable. It was a policy which made sense given the impossibility of uniting a divided population in any large-scale revolt. The aim was to create a 'second Vendée' in the South-east, as one of the leaders put it.

That purpose failed but the aim of disrupting normal life over larger areas of the South succeeded. The Jourdan Law introducing a more thorough and systematic form of conscription in September 1798 was a further powerful boost for the ranks of royalist brigandage. The requirement to serve in a disintegrating army in defence of an unpopular Republic, with all the personal upheaval and distress the absence of young men from farms could cause, was yet another challenge to the community, as it had been in 1793 in the Vendée. By 1800 violence, robbery, murder, the inefficiency of the law and the nervousness of judges all contributed to the deterioration of normal life. In addition, the line between politically motivated revolt and pure brigandage was becoming blurred, especially with the growing success of the authorities in capturing and executing the more notorious leaders such as Dominique Allier. The effect was to threaten the whole social and legal fabric rather than the political structure of the Revolution alone. Characteristics of southern life such as the vendetta, communal rivalry, ritualised violence, the protest against authority, especially distant, northern, centralised authority, all elements which were given a political dimension in the course of the Revolution, now seemed to be little more than an end in themselves, although caution is needed before judging them as entirely motiveless.

The Consulate might, therefore, still have a major problem on its hands in 1799–1800, and even as late as 1804 some localities were unsafe, but it was one which was largely now a matter of restoring respect for law and order, 'normal' times. In this the regime could count on the support of all those who welcomed a middle way between the political extremes of a return to republican Terror and an equally threatening popular royalism. The ruthless use of force on the one hand was combined, as had been done in the West, with inducements to informers and those who wished to give themselves up. At the same time local customs were respected or tolerated. In Provence this was not without deep misgivings by the officials at the potential and actual communal violence of many of these but it contributed to the impression of the restoration of normality. Much the same was true in all the insurrectionary regions: the application of force linked to respect for custom drew attention to the determination and efficiency of the new regime while at the same time removing what had been the principal source of most of the rebellions, the sense of injured local identity.

By 1802 *chouannerie* and brigandage had everywhere been suppressed.

This happy situation can mislead. Many of the elements which had given rise to rebellion remained. The emigration need no longer be taken seriously but individuals still tried to keep alive a framework of propaganda, information and future action. A number had sufficient commitment, even integrity, not to be bought off by the rewards of Bonapartist service. Men like Alexis de Noailles and Ferdinand de Bertier were to put together a network in 1810, the *Chevaliers de la foi*, which was to be a significant force as the Empire weakened. Remnants of the old Philanthropic Institutes remained in the South-west ready to be revived when the moment was right. In the South the leadership of displaced minor aristocracy and clerics still nursed their grievances and prepared for the next opportunity to stir up insurrection. Above all, many of the sources of popular royalism, especially in the Gard the communal rivalries between Catholic and Protestant, were a source of potential disorder once the firm administration of the Empire slipped. This more than anything else was the key to the situation. The Empire, and particularly the Emperor, could call on a considerable fund of loyalty from those whose careers and fortunes had been advanced by it, as well as all those who valued its respect for the gains of the Revolution within a framework of order and the guarantee of property. But in general support for the regime was conditional on its continuing success. That did not necessarily mean military success. Much more important was stability and prosperity at home. Partly that was tied to foreign policy but it was also linked in the Napoleonic system to administrative soundness and a far-reaching police network. As far as it was possible to be so in the circumstances of the early nineteenth century, Napoleonic France was a police state perpetually watching, reporting, suspecting anything which might deviate from the normal or represent a threat to order. The system rested on the actual or potential use of force. Loyalty was commanded.

From about 1809 that loyalty was starting to be strained. One reason was the breakdown of relations with the Papacy which resulted in Pius VII's exile and captivity in France. It was this which provoked the formation of the *Chevaliers de la foi*, but at popular level it offended religious feelings which had been carefully treated since the Concordat in 1801. The journey of the Pope into captivity and then out of it in 1814 aroused much popular emotion in Provence. Secondly the Empire's demands in taxation and conscription provoked fierce resentment.

The effect was the revival of the conditions in which popular royalism and its associated brigandage had flourished. The breakdown of the Empire under the pressure of military defeat and economic collapse was paralleled by the resurgence of brigandage fuelled by desertion and poverty. In these circumstances the mix of former seigneurs, *ancien régime* officials, and émigrés who had never ceased to scheme for the next opportunity could re-emerge for another round in the struggle.

Although we are mainly concerned with the Counter-Revolution in France the origins and motives behind it can be understood further by looking at the opposition to the French Revolution in the territories occupied by the revolutionary armies in 1792–3 and thereafter almost constantly from 1794–1814. The response to French policies and actions by the people of these territories shows many parallels with the motives behind popular Counter-Revolution inside France.

The beginning of the French Revolution was greeted abroad in various ways: by governments the normal attitude was to welcome French difficulties as an opportunity to pursue their own interests without the threat of interference from France; educated opinion on the other hand, with the exception of those like Burke in England who saw in it a challenge to the continuity of the political and social fabric, was generally enthusiastic at this triumph of the principles of individual freedom over what was popularly regarded as monarchical oppression. Paris soon had its community of foreign refugees and admirers involving themselves in the Revolution and pressing for similar movements in their own countries, which, they asserted, were only waiting to be rescued from tyranny.

Revolutionary governments and Assemblies before 1792 showed no inclination to spread the Revolution by force of arms although its principles were generally considered to have universal applicability. The mood of the first National Assembly was hostile to aggressive warfare, insisting instead on the fraternity of nations. In May 1790 it formally adopted a resolution condemning all wars of territorial conquest. When in April 1792 it did go to war it had to be cloaked in various declarations of revolutionary principle, for example by distinguishing between 'war on the castle' and 'peace to the cottage', and by pronouncing that the war was meant to bring liberty to oppressed peoples. In fact, at a very early stage the French followed a policy of annexation, justified by the entirely spurious doctrine of 'natural frontiers' in the case of Belgium and the Rhineland and supported by artificially created electoral majorities. By the beginning of 1793 France had annexed Belgium, even if briefly, as well as Nice, Savoy and a few other border territories. It seemed also to be about to annex some of the Rhineland. National interest had taken over even if it continued to be concealed behind declarations of revolutionary principle. 'The intrigues of the Court no longer direct the destinies [of France], but its policies are governed by the national interest in the pursuit of its enterprises', said the Foreign Minister in 1796. All pretence of 'liberation' was abandoned from 1793. Instead the occupied territories were treated as conquests.

The national interest was consequently interpreted to mean the ruthless exploitation of the resources of the conquered countries to support the war. The practice of making war pay for war was not, of course, confined to the French. What distinguished their practices was the systematic and organised stripping of the occupied territories' wealth. Under the Directory war became an end in itself, a means of sustaining the regime. But even before then, in the first invasion of Belgium in 1792–3 the efforts of Dumouriez to reassure the inhabitants by paying for supplies rather than by confiscations was swept aside by a policy which amounted to officially sanctioned looting, alongside private corruption and the depredations of unpaid and ill-fed troops. The exactions resumed when the French reinvaded Belgium in 1794 even though it was supposed to be on a more regulated scale. Nevertheless, hordes of French officials descended on the country making what were often outrageous and crippling demands, some of which took many years to pay off, 'Take all we can . . . strip it', ordered Carnot in July 1794. Much the same pattern was followed wherever the French armies went: the Rhineland was subjected to the depredations of officials and armies and individual generals in 1792–3 and again on its reinvasion in 1794, in spite of the protests of those French representatives who saw the inhabitants turning to sullen resentment and often plain brigandage as a protest, thus making the assimilation of the region into France more difficult. Bonaparte encouraged his army on the invasion of Italy in 1796 with the prospect of hitherto untapped resources to be looted. Peace treaties all included vast sums to be paid over to the French: 'I have brought you 100 million of these', said Sieyes, putting Dutch guilders on the Committee of Public Safety's table after the Treaty of the Hague in 1795. Allied countries like Holland in 1795, or the Cisalpine Republic in 1798, were as much a source of income as conquered ones. French exactions extended to works of art, justified on the grounds that only Paris, as the capital of the first nation of liberty, was worthy to give a home to the highest artistic achievements. Bonaparte included works of art in the treaty signed with Piedmont in April 1796. It set a pattern for the looting of the peninsula. 'What had become', asks Godechot, 'of the principles of the equality of man and the equality of peoples, of liberty, independence and national sovereignty?'

The territories invaded and occupied or annexed by the French were all deeply Catholic, with the exception of some Protestant enclaves in the Rhineland. To at least as great an extent as many parts of southern or western France Catholicism was a part of everyday communal life, present in the carnivals, festivals and customs of the region, genuinely popular. The French armies took with them into these regions the reputation of an anti-clerical revolution. Their troops did nothing to alter this opinion. They reflected the opinions and backgrounds from which they came and carried out the sort of desecration of churches, mocking of religious ceremonies and insults to priests which were a feature of that stage of the Revolution. In Belgium in particular some elements of the dechristianisation common in provincial France also took place such as the use of churches for the cult of Reason. Much the same happened in the Rhineland and Italy, although not the cult of Reason. The official side of French policy, the sequestration of monastic lands, the abolition of tithes, the spread of toleration for religious minorities, did little to compensate for the attacks on existing practice, and the persecution of the clergy which, in Belgium, included the death or deportation of a number of priests. The tithe was added to the rents with similar effects in the Rhineland, a region of high lease-holding, to the west of France; confiscated property mainly went to the bourgeoisie; and religious toleration for protestantism had little effect in the Rhineland where there had seldom been much friction, while the emancipation of the Jewish population from restrictions was not always popular.

Much might have been forgiven if the French had brought with them the benefits of efficient and honest government. Many of their agents tried to do so but under the pressures of military necessities and demands from the government in Paris they too often failed. The result was that administration appeared as an alien imposition in the hands of corrupt and incompetent individuals no more preferable, often worse, to what had existed before. This often went with an assumption of French superiority and a contempt for local custom and language which was deeply resented.

It is not surprising that the French were greeted hardly anywhere with popular enthusiasm or if they were it very soon soured. The Belgians welcomed the Austrians back in 1793 with some relief and the re-entry of the French into the country in the following year was preceded by a massive exodus. Collaborators with the French occupation in Europe were drawn from the small and unrepresentative number of the bourgeoisie who had done well out of land purchases and other opportunities to enrich themselves, just as in Belgium the foundations of industrialisation were laid during this period by those individuals enterprising enough to take advantage of such opportunities. For most people in occupied Europe, however, the revolutionary and Napoleonic period was disastrous. The increased demands for taxes, the requisitions, the looting and violence, the collapse of economic activity, and, in Belgium in September 1798, the imposition of conscription, meant only prolonged misery. Government could normally only be sustained by a strong military presence. When it was removed the administration collapsed. 'Strange errors, great misery and total failure', is how Kossman describes the period of French domination in Belgium.

Resistance, as in France, was in proportion to French military strength. In 1798 there was a revolt in Belgium, mainly in Flemish-speaking areas, provoked by conscription and made possible by the temporary weakness of French forces in the region. The French crushed it with severe reprisals. In the Rhineland there was no open revolt, merely passive resistance and widespread banditry. There was more serious resistance in the Tyrol and even more in southern Italy. In both these cases the terrain made rebellion easier to sustain, as it had been in western and southern France. But also the French had a limited military presence. In northern Italy, for example, there was a serious outbreak of anti-French violence in the Pavia region in May 1796 which Bonaparte punished with some severity. Thereafter, Lombardy remained quiet. A similar outbreak in Emilia was also summarily crushed. There was a much more serious outbreak of anti-French rioting at Verona in April 1797 but this also was crushed by Bonaparte who took the opportunity to end the independent Republic of Venice. In short, the revolts in northern Italy were only possible because of the brief distraction of the local French armies and lasted only as long as it took for these to return – a matter of days in effect. In Calabria, on the other hand, a landing by Cardinal Ruffo in February 1799, with a mere handful of followers, was able, because of the absence of any significant opposition, to launch a rebellion in the mountains of the area which eventually swept up thousands of followers, laid siege successfully to Naples, and advanced northwards into Tuscany where ferocious anti-French riots centred on the town of Arrezzo broke out in May and spread to nearby Sienna in the following month. Here also, that is in Tuscany, it was the news of French reverses and the rumour of an Austrian landing at Leghorn which was the occasion of the rebellion. The return of the French armies rapidly ended the disturbances at the end of the year.

The presence of adequate forces is therefore a key element in the success or failure of popular Counter-Revolution, as well as the character of the terrain. Southern Italy remained effectively ungovernable well into the next century in part at least because of this. The similarities with the problems of western and southern France go further. 'It is a complete Vendée', wrote a French general during the riots in the Rome region in 1799. He was referring to the religious character of the rebellions: Ruffo's army became known as the 'Sanfedists' on the grounds that they claimed to be fighting for the holy faith; in Arrezzo the rioters launched their attacks on the symbols of republicanism to the cry of 'Viva Maria'; in Rome and Sienna among other places Jews were singled out for savage treatment. Yet in Italy, far more than in Belgium or the Rhineland, the French were aware of the need to avoid offending religious feeling and, apart from the exile of the Pope and the granting of rights to the Jews, did so.

Cardinal Ruffo appealed not to outraged religious feeling but to a whole variety of local grievances and conflicts, among which were the poor for whom the French invasions and the destruction of the old order had done nothing. 'We do not want republics if we have to pay as before', said a Calabrian peasant. Ruffo's skill lay in the abolition of the more unpopular taxes and the hint of more to come, as well as the lure of loot. Support for the Revolution was identified with the traditional social enemies of the landless peasant and the urban poor: the rich, the bourgeois, the educated. The reforms carried out by revolutionary sympathisers were always deeply respectful of the rights of property and stopped short of the tax concessions and distribution of property which might have won over a broader area of support.

Yet just as in the counter-revolutionary areas of France it would be an error to single out any one cause or to see straightforward lines of division, rich against poor, for example, or clerical against anti-clerical. Ruffo himself, although he distributed religious symbols to the peasantry, was uneasy about uncontrolled popular religiosity. His own concern was to restore the authority of the prelates and the autonomy of the Church after the assaults on it not by the French and their local republican allies but by the Bourbon monarchy of Naples in the 1780s. He was able to draw on the support not just of the poor and landless but also of the rich and influential who had been affected by the reforms of the Bourbon monarchy. He therefore resisted any pressure to declare the abolition of feudalism on the grounds that it would alienate the wealthy. For the same reason he was apprehensive at the undisciplined hordes who began to flock to him and whose main concerns were localised grievances and rivalries. Counter-Revolution, in short, in southern Italy, as elsewhere in Europe, was less motivated by monarchist ideals or religious piety than a complex web of traditional hostilities of village and region, conflicts over land tenure and exploitation, economic changes, and the destabilising results of royal reform progammes which antagonised almost all social classes.

There is clearly much in common between popular Counter-Revolution in France and in the occupied territories but these similarities are in very broad and general terms. The details differed considerably from one area to another. The Revolution promised much but delivered little except to those people who were already substantial property-owners. The plight of the poor was made worse especially by the abolition or disruption of the monastic orders and with them their machinery of charity. The landless, the peasant with an insecure claim to property, or with interests in common rights, all found their position no better as a result of the French invasions. In fact, the French used the conquered territories to support the war and so imposed even greater burdens in taxes and other exactions, quite apart from the systematic stripping of works of art in Italy and Belgium. Even foreign Jacobins found themselves subordinated to the interests of French military necessity. In Belgium also the application of the Jourdan conscription law in 1799 provoked a very similar response to that of the Vendée: the 'War of the Peasants' in the autumn of 1798. The tactics employed, the targets of the attacks – municipal records, symbols of the revolution – and the strong religious element, all closely paralleled the rebellions in France.

Indeed, the religious feature is common to all popular counter-revolutionary risings. This was not unusual in Catholic countries but was probably given point by the reputation of the French for religious vandalism which preceded them in the countries they invaded. Apart from Italy where they took some pains to respect religious feeling, they did little to allay these fears. At the level of both the ordinary soldier and the senior officers sacrilege, blasphemy and wanton destruction offended local feeling in regions where Catholicism was woven into the cultural pattern of everyday life.

Yet there is no reason to suppose that this alone would have produced revolt. The Rhineland, for example, saw no great rebellion, as distinct from one brigandage or refusal to co-operate with the occupiers in the administration. The Sanfedists included the religious and irreligious yet almost all adopted the various religious slogans and rallying cries. The place of religion in the popular Counter-Revolution in the occupied territories is, in the end, much the same as in France. Religion was the framework within which the mass of the population lived their lives and expressed their thoughts and aspirations. There is no need to look for a religious motivation for popular revolt, although this might occur when religious practice, as part of popular culture, was attacked. Societies under stress expressed their grievances and demands in religious form. The origins of that stress were rooted in violent change imposed from outside by urban influences, economic pressures, military conscription and material requisitions, or the imposition of alien institutions, all of which struck at the cultural integrity and traditions of communities without any compensating advantage in the form of tax relief or land distribution. The Age of Revolution was also, as Blanning points out, the Age of Counter-Revolution throughout Europe.

5

The Bourbons Restored

As the allied armies slowly advanced into France early in 1814, every step contested by Napoleon, it was by no means clear what regime should succeed the Empire. The triumph of the Counter-Revolution was not at all assured. The comte de Vitrolles, a Provençal nobleman who in 1814 took it on himself to plead the cause of the Bourbons among the allies, found that neither they nor the parts of eastern France he travelled through had much enthusiasm for the exiles. The allies, in fact, had no fixed or agreed views on the issue. The British, from the time of their entry into the war in 1793, had consistently maintained the principle that whatever regime was established in France must have the consent of the majority of the people, be stable and peaceful. In practice this had come to mean a constitutional monarchy, although as Vitrolles realised, this was dependent on a British parliament and public opinion which was not particularly sympathetic to the former monarchy. In the absence of any clear indication of support inside France the British were unwilling to commit themselves. The allies took a similar line. 'Let France declare itself', was the core of Metternich's reply. Vitrolles was shocked to find that the Tsar was even talking of a Republic. There was little evidence in the allied camp in 1814 of that later emphasis on 'legitimacy' which was to underpin the actions of the Holy Alliance. That was a concept still to be given wider acceptance by Talleyrand although it had, as we saw, been raised by Louis XVIII and Artois in 1804 in their circular to the powers as the answer to Napoleon's creation of a new dynasty.

In fact, there was no real alternative to a Bourbon restoration but French public opinion had to indicate some support for the policy. Royalists asserted that in 1814 the Bourbons were all but forgotten by the French people – as little known, claimed Chateaubriand, as 'the children of the Emperor of China'. This was exaggerated, although most contemporaries agreed that outside a few nobility, clergy and wealthy bourgeois there was widespread ignorance. What they usually meant, however, was ignorance about the details of the royal family. Such details were important to royalists but scarcely so to the mass of the population. It was highly unlikely that the existence of the Bourbons was unknown since there were a number of ex-royalists in the Napoleonic administration, such as Pasquier, the Prefect of the Paris police in 1810, and royalist plots had hardly been interrupted during the Empire even if most had been of little importance since 1804. There had nevertheless been a fresh outbreak of royalist conspiracy in 1812–13. There also remained a substantial popular base in parts of the Midi on which the *Chevaliers de la foi*, for example, could attempt to build as the Empire's difficulties increased.

The first indications of support for the Bourbons came from the South-west. In the East it was unwise, while the allied success hung in the balance, to make too early a declaration of royalist loyalty. The key event was in Bordeaux, a city hard-hit by the blockade. Here on 12 March the mayor, comte Lynch, gave way to pressure as well as to his own estimate of the way events were moving, to hand over the city to one of Wellington's commanders. Bordeaux thus became endowed with the honour of being the first city to welcome back the Bourbons. More important was the fact that it persuaded Wellington that there was a strong element of Bourbon support in the country. Elsewhere the outcome was still finely balanced: a royalist demonstration in Paris on 31 March attracted little attention. But on the same day Paris surrendered and Talleyrand persuaded the Tsar that the Senate was willing to recall the Bourbons. Napoleon abdicated on 6 April and the next day Louis was declared 'king of the French'.

This title was part of a wider problem, that is, the terms on which the monarchy should be restored. No one of any political significance thought that a restoration should or could take place as if nothing had happened. It was taken for granted that the restored monarchy should be a constitutional one – it had after all been an article of faith among the émigrés and all royalists of whatever shade of opinion that France had always had a constitution which had been corrupted and finally ignored by the later monarchy. The issue was the nature and title, not the fact, of this constitution. It was a question which was to dog the whole of the Restoration period. Vitrolles refers to the variety of opinions in Paris as to the type of constitution possible: 'each thought of it in his own terms according to his leanings'.

The Senate which recalled the Bourbons had their own view of the constitutional place of the Crown, which they set down in a document part of whose purpose was to safeguard their status: it imposed the constitution on a monarchy 'recalled' by a Senate whose members were to retain their positions on a hereditary basis; Louis was 'king of the French' and was referred to as 'Louis-Stanislas-Xavier brother of the last king'. In short, there was no recognition of Louis XVII. Moreover, the throne was made dependent on prior acceptance of the constitution. This was the constitution, a closer forerunner of the 1830 Orléanist version, which Artois found when he entered Paris on 14 April to enormous acclaim and his own mixture of surprise and sobbed emotion. It was wholly unacceptable. Only a compromise suggested by Fouché enabled the Senate and Artois to suspend this version pending the arrival of Louis. In the meantime Artois acted as Lieutenant-General of the Kingdom, an arrangement which gave the opportunity for some die-hard monarchists to assert their social and political claims, 'emerging from beneath the paving, convinced they were conquerors and wanting to show it', according to Mme du Boigne, whose journal provides gossipy observations on the social scene. Their activities were enough to cause some early resentments to develop in those who saw their positions threatened.

These individuals who attached themselves to Artois were, however, by no means representative of royalist opinion which covered a considerable range of political views and attitudes towards the monarchy. In effect, most of France was monarchist, or at least prepared to support any regime which offered peace and stability. In 1797, after all, there had been substantial electoral support for a constitutional monarchy. The more extreme royalists, the heirs of the 'pures' and of Coblenz, formed the elements of what came to be called after 1816 the 'ultras'. But they represented only part of the counter-revolutionary tradition, certainly not all of it, and even they varied almost as widely in political complexion and background as the Counter-Revolution itself had done. There was thus no question of a political party, although the outlines of one came to develop in the course of the Restoration. There was no clearly agreed programme on the body of doctrine which would have made it possible; neither was there any great consistency in their approach to the issues of the day. They did not represent a homogenous social class: Piet, the man in whose house many ultra deputies met in 1816, was a lawyer, and others ranged from a Montmorency, one of the oldest families in France, to Corbières, son of a peasant. They were not all unrepentant and unreconstructed émigrés: many had served in the imperial administration; large numbers of others had returned from exile long before 1814. In the course of the Restoration they were also to divide and fragment even further.

Nevertheless, there remained a great deal of continuity between ultra politics and the world of the aristocratic emigration and the Counter-Revolution. There was a broad consistency of principle if not always of practice. The first of these was an attitude to monarchy which saw it not so much as a convenient system of government as an object of personal loyalty. This in part accounts for the belief among the returned émigrés that the Bourbons were forgotten when they meant that the names and relationships of the family were unfamiliar in France. This was almost inconceivable to an ultra. This devotion enabled them to overlook the only too obvious faults of the royal family, for the most part an extremely unattractive collection of individuals. It was not a rational view of monarchy; it was for example poles apart from the views of politicians such as Constant, or Guizot and Royer-Collard for whom it was more an institutional device, a safeguard of a certain type of social order. This personal aspect of royalism could help ultras to overcome the many disappointments of the Restoration. 'Long live the king just the same', as the ultra newspaper, *Le Drapeau Blanc*, echoing one of the deputies, said after the dissolution of the *Chambre Introuvable* in 1816. It was a concept which had also sustained royalists during their years of frustration and exile.

This approach to royalty meant that tampering with the monarchy through the artificial and human devices of a written constitution could seem inappropriate, almost blasphemous. This view, however, was rare in France, being more a feature of the conservatism of Metternich's central Europe. No one seriously doubted the need for a constitution in France. The limitation on royal power, or any power, was deeply rooted in all shades of counter-revolutionary as well as revolutionary thinking. The Bourbons themselves accepted this, as the numerous declarations since 1791 had made clear. 'Pastry made of the finest constitutional flour', was how Beugnot described Louis XVIII. Artois, himself to be the future hope of the hard-line ultras, also accepted a constitutional form of monarchy. But it had to be a constitution granted by, not imposed upon, the Crown. It also had to make clear the continuity of monarchy not just in terms of the numbering of the king but in the tradition of the institution. This was the burden of the Declaration of Saint-Ouen issued by Louis on 3 May. Many royalists argued that no break at all should be implied: any constitution should be in the nature of a reform of the old, 'The Old Regime made rational', as one of them put it. It may be remembered that Louis XVIII himself had shocked Lord Macartney in 1795 by extolling the virtues of the old constitution which, he claimed, merely needed some refurbishment. Vitrolles, as we have seen, understood and accepted the need for a constitution. He had been one of the three who drew up the Declaration of Saint-Ouen and himself drafted a lengthy proposal of his own version. However, he felt that the word 'constitution' should not be used because it was tainted by association with Republics and Revolutions – the term 'Royal Charter' was better – and that it should be made clear that it was merely an extension, a reform, of the traditional, pre-existing, constitution of the old monarchy. Therefore only the changes needed to be mentioned. Change was acceptable when it was an organic part of the human condition, the fruit of experience, not the consequence of the application of reason. Such views in various forms were widespread among ultras but certainly did not preclude severe limitations on royal power, indeed they implied them. In some circumstances they were to outdo the liberals in this respect.

How these limitations were to be expressed in institutional form was a key area of difference not just from liberals but within the ranks of the ultras as well. They were also perfectly capable of accommodating much political flexibility. The conflict between the ultra *Chambre Introuvable* and the government in 1816 was to drive Chateaubriand to produce 'The Monarchy according to the Charter', a defence of constitutionalism through a parliamentary system. This was not new, even within ultra ranks, although his literary fame and the timing of its appearance made it a best-seller. Moreover, the parliamentarism of the ultras wavered according to their strength in the Chamber. Nevertheless, Chateaubriand built his argument on familiar ultra principles, those of continuity. The constitution of 1814 was merely the development of old forms, the building on old foundations: 'no political changes can be securely established except on the base of the political order which they have succeeded'. Chateaubriand went further than many ultras would have thought appropriate, however, as well as being possibly inconsistent by arguing that the *ancien régime* was dead: 'Facts are facts. Whether the government which has been destroyed was good or bad, it has been destroyed. . . . Let us always deplore the fall of the former government, that admirable system whose antiquity alone was its praise; but after all. . . .'

The ultra approach to the constitution was, therefore, not a rigid defence of an unchanging order. The constitution should, however, reflect certain fundamental principles of human conduct and history. What these were represented another of the general characteristics of the ultra mind. Even though the ultras were for the most part men of the eighteenth century, they drew on many of the same sources as the Revolution they rejected, had been marked by 1814 by its course, and had adopted some of its institutions and methods. They had also been influenced, in some respects transformed, by the intellectual consequences of Romanticism, the religious revival and, in the case of the émigrés, the experience of exile. Some, according to Baldensperger, had discovered a sense of nationalism while in exile, reinforced by Romanticism. This can probably be overstated. What still mattered most to the ultra were the values of the regime and society he served. 'Nation' meant, said the marquis de Castelbajac in 1815, 'not the soil to which I am fixed under the shameful laws of usurpation and despotism, but the country of my ancestors, with their legitimate government, government which grants me protection by virtue of my obedience to the laws, and which I am obliged to serve with honour and loyalty.' Nationalism in its modern sense was not yet a feature of the Right. The reappearance in 1814 of numbers of former émigrés in the military uniform of France with ranks they had done nothing to earn, who had often fought against the Empire in the service of its enemies and boasted of it, was one of the more insensitive aspects of the First Restoration which made it easier for Napoleon to find allies during the Hundred Days.

If the growth of a new-style patriotism had left many ultras behind, the religious revival, and the course of a Revolution which had become anti-clerical deeply marked the Counter-Revolution. The eighteenth-century sceptics had become, or frequently appeared so, deeply pious; none more so than Artois himself, moved in that direction by his dying mistress in 1804. The king-martyr Louis XVI, the apparently inexorable descent of the Revolution into Terror and bloodshed, and finally the restoration of the monarchy when it had scarcely seemed possible even to hope, all gave substance to a belief that Providence was working in favour of the Bourbons. The Restoration, it was argued, was the judgement of Providence. The religious dimension to the state, government and society was central to ultra thinking. One of the more contentious issues in the Charter was the place it gave to the Catholic religion, and the resulting compromise was never acceptable to those ultras who felt that merely describing it as the religion of the State was an inadequate definition. The union of Throne and Altar, the divine origin of monarchy and authority, the sacred nature of social hierarchy were fundamental to most ultra thinking. From this there followed the need to moralise society by giving a special place to the Church, especially in the educational system and by laws protecting the Church's doctrine and ceremonies. Here, for example, is de Bertier in 1825 speaking in the Chamber in support of a law on sacrilege: 'It cannot be doubted that the Church has no need of the power of the State, but the power of the State has need of it . . . because when there is no longer any religion, there is no longer any need of obedience or respect for the laws . . . the duty and interest of kings is therefore to defend religion.' Bertier by this stage did not reflect the views of all ultras, but the general view that the State needed a revivified Church with sufficient wealth and prestige to sustain its work would not have found any dissent. In spite of the Restoration's considerable success in strengthening the Church many ultras continued to detect too much of the revolutionary and imperial spirit surviving in the legal and social system.

That spirit needed to be rooted out through religious means because in the mind of the more extreme ultras the Revolution was more than just a political event. They saw it as a divine retribution on a faithless nation led astray by a conspiracy of free-thinkers, freemasons and Protestants, corrupted by Voltairian scepticism. That analysis may not have been articulated in such crude terms but it was the essence of the thinking of the more hard-line and unforgiving members of the far Right. The most vigorous expression was found in the works of de Maistre and Bonald, not widely read in 1815 but representing some of the attitudes of the ultras. The Revolution according to de Maistre was the visitation of God on France as a punishment for its sins, a necessary use of Evil in order to prepare the way through chastisement for the expiation of those sins. The Restoration therefore should be more than a mere form of government but the channel through which the last vestiges of France's contamination could be expunged and the unity and harmony restored which had been broken by the centuries of sectarian factionalism, the sapping of the roots of Christian order and due obedience to authority. The simple restoration of the *ancien régime* was not enough. A new unity had to be created based on religion, authority and hierarchy.

Tradition, emotion, prejudice, the group rather than a fragmenting individualism were the important concepts: a rejection of the eighteenth century. Society and sovereignty gave force and meaning to each other, drawing together an otherwise meaningless collection of individuals and allowing Providence to make itself manifest. Authority ran through the whole part of the hierarchy, exercising itself in various ways from top to bottom. Its most dramatic symbol, suggested de Maistre, was the executioner. If anything distinguished the early nineteenth-century liberal from the extreme royalist it was this emphasis on the group, on authority and on tradition. The Revolution, on the other hand, had been a conscious, deliberate rejection of the past. It also became anti-clerical, not by design, but by political compulsion strengthened by gradually opposing principles. The social differences between the heirs of the Revolution and Empire on the one side and the Counter-Revolution on the other probably counted for little if anything at all. They belonged to that notable class of wealth and property which had begun the revolutionary process and which in the end was to govern nineteenth-century France. In 1814, however, and for much of the Restoration, in terms of ideology they belonged to two different worlds. How, and on what terms, were they to be brought together?

Louis was better able than his brother to weave his way through their conflicting claims. Unaffected by the romantic piety to which so many other émigrés, including Artois, had succumbed, he retained the detached scepticism of the eighteenth century, reinforced in his case by a certain idleness, an absence of any deeply held principles and a capacity to act a part. He felt strongly about very little except the dignity of his position, which he sustained by a passionate interest in the tiniest details of court dress and protocol, and the legitimacy of his claim to the throne. Above all, he understood, as Artois never did, the realities of the problem he was faced with: of bringing together two nations. The means of doing this was the Charter, as the constitution came to be called. It was the basic document of the Restoration period, essentially a compromise between the two strands of the property-owning political classes, the revolutionary and counter-revolutionary. The committee which compiled it represented both of these. It was granted to the nation in the nineteenth year of the king's reign, thus underlining the continuity of the Crown's claims to legitimacy. In many respects it bore close similarities with the British model as it existed at that time, and with which the king had some sympathy. It gave equal weight in political affairs to the king, for example the power to initiate legislation, dissolve the Chamber, appoint ministers, create peers for the Upper Chamber. Compared to previous constitutions, such as that of 1791, the electorate was tiny, in effect only a fragment of that notable class, the amalgamation of wealth of whatever source, which had emerged from the Revolution. However, the constitution reflected most of the general principles of moderate liberalism at the time and most considered it as an acceptable compromise, a working basis for continuing discussion and political development, to be amended according to taste, rather than a fixed and unchangeable law. There was nothing wrong with this as long as debate could be conducted within a framework of political trust and goodwill. Those were to be diminishing commodities. In the end the policies and attitudes of Crown, ministers and politicians, and the continuing gulf between the two political traditions, undermined the reassurance which the Charter had offered to the revolutionary tradition in France.

In one very important respect, among all the others, the Charter was a deep disappointment to many ultras: it retained the centralised structure of government and administration which had emerged from the Revolution and Empire. Ultras might, on the whole, agree on the concepts of an ordered, hierarchical and traditional society bound together by obedience and religious piety. That was the moral dimension to society which in other contexts allowed royalism to develop its social concern. On much else, however, there was little agreement and even considerable tension. But there was at least one other area of common ground: ultras and even many moderate royalists felt a deep attachment to the traditions and rights of the old provinces. A restoration of the old Estates or at least some form of local Assembly was attractive to a number of them. A decentralised France was a cherished royalist principle for many years to come. In that way power would be limited by various intermediate bodies and the provincial gentry given proper scope for the development of their influence free from the corrupting interference of Paris. Decentralisation was therefore a mix of traditionalism, provincial resentments and local power-politics, as well as a certain romantic antiquarianism in some cases. In practice no government, royalist or otherwise, felt able to concede it. The centralised and uniform system of administration inherited from the Revolution and Empire placed a degree of power in the hands of government which none of them was prepared to abandon. There were other reasons: decentralisation too often meant not the benevolent exercise of power by a disinterested aristocracy and a defence against the abuses of central government but its misuse for private ends and especially against local minorities. For these groups the true protector was the central government. Nowhere was this more evident than in the Midi.

The political turbulence of the Midi was compounded by a resentment of distant northern dominance and officials, and in the south-east long-standing religious conflicts and rivalries. The reception of the duc d'Angoulême in Toulouse in 1814 and again in 1815 had much to do with provincial resentment of the north. That is how Rémusat, whose father was sent as Prefect in 1815, assessed it. He found there a pleasure in defying Paris, especially a Paris which seemed barely royalist, and 'where influences suspect to all royalists restricted the king's politics and liberty'. There was talk of a 'Kingdom of Occitania' which would represent true royalism better. This was supported in the Toulouse region by a close-knit, conservative, cautious nobility, of whom Villèle, the future ultra leader in the Chamber, was an example. It dominated local politics. The fiery outbursts which characterised these politics, although soon over, gave no confidence in its capacity to provide stable and even-handed government. This was even more true of the Gard.

Provincial resentments, a sense of the betrayal of ideals, were also bound up with more material grievances. Royalists who had lost property and relations, who had spent years in exile, risked lives in popular insurrections, expected some recognition of a loyalty sustained at such cost over so long. The issue of lost lands was, at a national level, the most contentious and had been the most difficult over which to make concessions. Uncertainty over them was to bedevil much of Restoration politics. The failure to deal with the question created uncertainty amongst the purchasers and resentment among those who had lost. They felt that the Crown had capitulated on this as on so much else to the pressures of revolutionary and imperial politicians. The royalists, in the immediate term, also had high hopes of recovering lost positions in administration, the judiciary and government. This could be partially satisfied at a national level although the sight of émigrés resuming their broken military careers in ranks they ill-deserved, alongside distinguished Napoleonic soldiers, caused resentment and derision. Numbers of royalists were also given office as prefects, ministers and judges, which they frequently filled with distinction.

Yet there was simply not enough to go round even if a wholesale purge of imperial officials had been possible or desirable. The result was a sense of frustration mainly at the middle and lower levels of provincial royalism. The Restoration of 1814 could thus be seen as a monstrous betrayal, the Charter a deception, a breach of principles and tradition, and Louis XVIII the 'crowned Jacobin'. An alternative focus could be found in the comte d'Artois or his elder son the duc d'Angoulême.

Artois was the main hope of ultracism. His apartments in the Pavillon de Marsan (a wing of the Louvre) became the centre of a virtually alternative government, the *cabinet vert* (green was the colour of his livery), with its own network of agents through the provinces, secretive and conspiratorial. Artois' colours became the outward sign of loyalty to his system. His more attractive and surprisingly youthful appearance increased his appeal although his character was potentially a disaster for the monarchy. He prided himself on his inflexible adherence to principle and during the First Restoration surrounded himself with individuals redolent of Coblenz. Here was a focal point of all those who felt aggrieved for material or other reasons, who saw in the monarchy as restored by Louis XVIII a denial of all that the Counter-Revolution had stood for. This opposition was not always self-interested. In the case of some members of the *Chevaliers de la foi*, like de Bertier or Montmorency, it could be based on a deeply held religious faith even if out of touch with the new scheme of things. Their vision of a society bound together by mutual responsibility and consideration could lead, in other hands, to a social Catholicism. Such an element had been found in the concern of the southern Catholic royalist at the condition of the textile workers in the hands of the Protestant merchants. An orderly hierarchical society could be a safeguard against injustice for the poor.

The less pleasant face of ultracism was, however, more evident in the first years of the Restoration and demonstrated the hollowness of some of its loftier claims. Royalism had a strong popular base in the Midi compounded of southern separateness, economic discontents, religious divisions. Bordeaux was, as we have seen, the first city to declare for the Bourbons, but Toulouse also gave an emotional (and therefore misleading) welcome to the Restoration. Here, the politically inflexible royalists, the romanticising of the past, were reinforced by a claim to be the 'capital of the Midi', a bastion of southern traditional values against northern materialism and Parisian centralism. Ultra-royalism dominated the city and made the work of the centrally appointed Prefect virtually impossible in 1814–15. Popular royalism was easily turned to violence against anyone who might try to restrain the excesses of the ultras. More intractable and deeply rooted violence was found in the Gard as the former leaders of Counter-Revolution such as Froment emerged in 1814 to claim their rewards and to try to reverse the Protestant dominance established in 1790. The failure of these survivors of the Counter-Revolution to displace the Protestants, their resentment at the inadequacy of their treatment, especially compared to the upper levels of the local notables, meant both the perpetuation of religious conflict and the organisation of opposition to the central government which had 'betrayed' the principles of pure royalism. During the First Restoration these elements, organised in a *société royale*, disrupted local Protestant administrations and looked to Artois for leadership and recompense for their loyalty.

The ingredients for disorder and discontent were therefore already present in the South when Bonaparte landed at Cannes in March 1815. Only Angoulême succeeded in raising a force to try and check his advance but at La Palud a truce was arranged with General Gilly which allowed it to disband and Angoulême made his way to Spain. He left behind him in the south a sort of underground administration, at the same time hoping that sufficient numbers could be recruited to swell his forces in order to allow the royalists to liberate the South unaided by the allies. In Toulouse secret companies (*secrets*) were organised to take over in the event of Bonaparte's defeat. Before Angoulême's departure for Spain a 'shadow' administration and 'army', often of dubious elements, had been set up. The individuals who followed him to Spain developed their ideas, theoretical and practical, for the system of government to be restored in the reconquered South, and ultimately nationally. The new Restoration would avoid the mistakes of the first by an assertion of the principles of provincial autonomy under aristocratic control, of hierarchy and a strong Church, Catholic royalism in the ascendant. The base for this would be, initially, a 'Kingdom of the Midi' or 'Kingdom of Aquitaine' with Angoulême as viceroy. Angoulême played no active part in all this theorising, and certainly as a Bourbon centralist had no practical interest. It was nevertheless the policy which the administrators appointed by him, and their Catholic notable and popular supporters, attempted to pursue.

The Hundred Days were critical in the development of the politics of the Restoration. The confusion and power vacuum which followed the defeat of Bonaparte gave the southern royalists their opportunity to establish a microcosm of the type of society they wanted to see in France as a whole. It was to show the darker unattractive side of royalism to be set alongside its more appealing features such as the occasional social concern. As the Bonapartist generals withdrew undisciplined royalist gangs settled old scores: in Marseilles disorders went on from June to September; in Toulon the gangs had the free run of an ungoverned city; in Avignon the Bonapartist general Brune was murdered while being conducted back to Paris. In Toulouse the secret companies, the Angoulême-appointed Prefect Limayrac, and the royalist military commander de Rougé successfully contested the authority of Paris until late August. In the middle of the month the Paris-appointed military commander, Ramel, was murdered in particularly atrocious circumstances by a member of the secret companies, connived at by the authorities with the object of demonstrating the popular support behind the concept of a 'Kingdom of the Midi'. Violent though events were in Toulouse they soon died down as local figures of the stature of Villèle turned to developing their ambitions through Paris and moderated their ultracism.

The Gard was a different matter. Here the roots of violence were deeper than in Toulouse or anywhere else in the South. Local sectarian differences, a developed network of Catholic royalism, and the leadership of a resentful notable class ensured a longer and more intractable future for ultra royalism. The White Terror which raged through the South in 1815 built on previous outbreaks to be avenged and the judiciary and administration were too corrupt and biased to exercise any effective control. The Prefect sent in July by the royal government soon fell under the influence of local royalism which had made out of the administration, supported by the National Guard and police, a sort of government-in waiting looking to Artois and the Pavillon de Marsan for a system acceptable to ultra opinion, free of the compromises of Louis XVIII. As commander-in-chief of the National Guards throughout France Artois was the centre of a network of corresponding companies. The key to the success of royalist plans to hold the fort until Artois' succession to the throne was prolonged resistance against the pressures from Paris and eventually a decentralised structure of government for France as a whole.

That was to be disappointed. From 1817 the central government began to reassert its control although it was always challenged by a southern popular royalism able to take advantage of the special conditions of the Midi and, in the 1820s, royalist conflicts in Paris. Nevertheless, for all its enduring strengths, Midi royalism had many weaknesses. It was based on local conditions such as, in the Gard, the survival of sectarian conflicts of no national relevance; in some cases, for example Toulouse, it was hot-headed and impulsive and therefore ephemeral, justifying some of the stereotypes of the Midi current in the North. In both these cases it was marginal to the mainstream of Bourbon royalism and most royalists, even ultras, at a national level were uneasy at its excesses. It was out of step also because it rested on the success of provincial decentralisation which was at variance with the policies of central government, pursued by all wings of royalism when they were actually in power whatever they might have said when in opposition or merely at the level of local politics. Centralisation brought the successful politician power and opportunities as well as the capacity to act against local particularism. It was something no government was ever likely to abandon. Decentralisation was seen as the key to the survival of the influence and values of the Catholic provincial aristocracy although in its turn it would be threatened by the structure of elections bequeathed by the Revolution. In the end the old liberties of the provinces remained more theoretical than practical and ultimately a romantic dream, enshrined in literature and newspaper titles. No ultra-type state was really possible in the sort of centralised bureaucratic parliamentary system retained by the Restoration. That did not stop them trying to achieve something of the kind even if not as complete as the ambitions of the Gard royalists.

The Hundred Days gave the ultras their best opportunity under Louis XVIII to press for concessions at a national level. The reaction against Bonaparte and the intimidation, especially in the White Terror in the south, of the small electorate, resulted in the *Chambre Introuvable*, a large ultra presence of 78 per cent of the Chamber in September 1815. There was also a purge of between 50,000–80,000 officials, far more thorough-going than in 1814 although a change of political complexion rather than of social class. The opportunity was used for some vindictive measures against Bonapartists, of which the best known was the execution of Marshal Ney. It was also the occasion for some fiery speeches which parallel the events in the Midi and like them illustrate the unattractive face of ultracism. 'We need chains, executioners, death-sentences. Only death can terrify their accomplices and end their plots', said La Bourdonnaye. Trinquelaque, from Nîmes and with a record of prominence in popular Catholic royalism in the Gard, called for the re-establishment of hanging for seditious utterances: 'We must strike swiftly. Such punishment is difficult with the guillotine, a complicated instrument, large and awkward to move. The old method had none of these disadvantages. You can find a piece of string anywhere, everyone has some in his pocket, and everywhere there's a nail, a beam and tree branch to fix it to.'

The setting up of special courts and laws against seditious writings also reflected ultra thinking, as did increases in ecclesiastical salaries. This had some value. Lachèze's justification for it has force: 'It isn't easy to restore a Nation's morality and, if it is possible to achieve it, it can only be done through the influence of religion. To secure that valuable end through that influence we must have good priests, we must lift them above the level of poverty, we must show them that their virtues and services are valued, we must finally force people to have recourse to them at the great moments of their lives.' It is the last point, however, which distinguishes the ultra case from the moderate royalist. Lachèze was arguing for the restoration of clerical control over the *état civil*, that is, registration of births, deaths and marriages. The Chamber also abolished divorce.

All this brought the Chamber into conflict with the king and the government in the course of which the ultra majority began to develop something like a theory of parliamentary sovereignty, of which Chateaubriand's book was an example. This had its value during these early years of constitutional monarchy. But the ultras were no more consistent in this than their doctrinaire opponents who at this stage were emphasising the equal place of the Crown in the constitution. They adapted constitutional principles to the political circumstances of the moment. The ultras in fact were always caught in a series of dilemmas. Some of these at the level of provincial popular royalism have been mentioned above. At the national and parliamentary level also they found themselves faced with numerous contradictions. If they emphasised freedom and the rights of groups, the importance of checks on power – central power, royal power – there were always limits to these freedoms. Some ultras such as Lamennais were, it is true, to move on from the liberties of hierarchical groups to the claims of the poor; but in the Restoration period, especially in 1816, this was a long way from the thoughts of the *Chambre Introuvable* as a whole. Rémusat found them muddled and hypocritical and because of this unable to draw on the support of otherwise liberal opinion outside the Chamber or inside it. When, after 1816, they were in a minority in the Chamber and were denouncing 'arbitrary' government, 'one would have needed to believe', writes Rémusat, 'that they had forgotten that it was they who the previous year had encouraged arbitrary measures, called for severity and given the authorities, which they had found deficient, the means of action which they now reproached them for having used.' Events after 1820 and in 1830 were to show that the ultras were not the party of freedom. There were limits also in the extent to which they were prepared to push the claim for parliamentary sovereignty: there was no question of rejecting the budget; or of increasing the popular base of parliament by widening the electorate and so possibly diluting its landed character. Chateaubriand did not represent the bulk of ultra opinion.

The dissolution of the Chamber by Louis XVIII in September 1816 was an effort to restore less heated politics. In the new Chamber the ultras were reduced to 92 members. The tone of government was set by Decazes who defined his objectives as 'making the nation royalist and royalism national'. The ultras were on the defensive and in their frustration may possibly have turned not just to the promotion of parliamentary sovereignty but to more dubious courses such as the 'Waterside Conspiracy', a supposed plot to kidnap some ministers. In fact there were more hopeful signs that the ultras were developing the outlines of a political party with a degree of parliamentary discipline, a press, a broad set of principles resting on Throne and Altar royalism, and a popular base. There is a rough similarity to a type of English Toryism and it is worth reminding ourselves that the English party system was also at this time still in an early stage of its development with just such vague sets of common principles. What was missing in France, among much else, was the security and continuity of the English political system. Time, thought, Rémusat, might have developed the ultras into a party of parliamentary government. This may have been optimistic but in any case in February 1820 the assassination of the duc de Berry, Artois' younger son and the hope for the continuation of the dynasty, forced the dismissal of Decazes and a lurch to the Right which was to set the tone of the 1820s. The result was an increasing sense of insecurity among those on the Left and the Centre who otherwise supported the monarchy.

Yet this can be overstated. Decazes was already shifting to the Right before February 1820 and the policies of his successor, Richelieu, were a long way from satisfying ultra opinion. The succession of Villéle as effective head of the government in December 1821 marked a more decisive move Right. Villèle was a former mayor of Toulouse, a *Chevalier de la foi*, leader of the ultras in the Chamber, virtually the appointment of Artois. Measures were taken to strengthen the role of the Church in the education system, further restrictions were imposed on the press, military intervention was undertaken in Spain in support of the king. But this scarcely amounted to the ultra programme. In spite of his ultra credentials Villèle was not the stuff of which extreme royalism was made. There was much of the peasant about him, says Fourcassié: materialistic, realistic, a shrewd and successful manager of his estates, typical of many of the minor Toulousain nobility from which he came. He was a long way from the romanticism of much ultra thinking and had no sympathy with the literary outpourings of Chateaubriand. His dismissal of Chateaubriand (June 1824) in circumstances which the latter found humiliating turned into a major breach in the royalist ranks. The election early in 1824 of the *Chambre Retrouvée* with its large ultra majority also made division more likely both because of the problems of controlling it and because of dissatisfaction with Villèle.

It would, however, be wrong to regard the Bourbon Restoration as already doomed to failure by 1824 when Louis XVIII was succeeded by Artois. There was no question, outside a handful on the far Left, of overthrowing it. It was more secure than before, France was once more a full part of the Concert of Europe, its parliamentary system well established, its administration honest, and competent. Even among the more extreme heirs of the Counter-Revolution there was no intention of overturning it. What they had not abandoned was that Throne and Altar politics which under Charles X was to appear a sinister conspiracy against the constitution, especially when it was combined with suspicions of the king and measures apparently aimed at the section of the notable class which had benefited from the Revolution. In the end, however, it took quite remarkable political misjudgement, not to say stupidity, to destroy the Restoration monarchy but the roots of those errors lie also in the dilemmas and conflicts of ultra politics.

6

Charles X

The reign of Charles X lasted for just six years. It is easy to see it as a downhill slide into inevitable revolution. Nothing could be further from the truth. There was little that was inevitable about the fall of the Bourbon monarchy – the opponents of Charles' policies were a long way from being revolutionaries and until almost the last moment some compromise was possible. Charles came to the throne in an atmosphere of general goodwill, an overwhelmingly royalist Chamber, and an opposition to the dynasty which undoubtedly existed but which was unorganised, unfocused and small.

In any analysis of the disaster which overtook the Bourbon monarchy a central place has to be given to the character of Charles X as much as to the failings of the monarchy itself. He started with some considerable personal advantages, especially compared to Louis XVIII, which are by no means to be discounted: a charm and amiability (in sharp contrast to almost all his relations), a distinguished, even 'kingly', appearance, and loyalty to old friends which has some merit even if the friends could have been more wisely chosen. None of this was possessed by the graceless, rude, repulsive and selfish old king: 'a mediocre character . . . falseness and hypocrisy' were some of Rémusat's comments. Yet Louis left the restored monarchy in a strong, even popular, position. In part this was because of his very infirmities: his laziness, lack of grasp of detail, boredom with administrative routine, and physical immobility meant that he left politics to his ministers as long as he was accorded the respect due to his kingship. In any difficulties he was happy enough to sacrifice friends to whom he had once given every sign of eternal devotion. All this was no bad thing in a constitutional monarch at a time of uneasy and tense political transition. In practice, whatever the ambiguities of the Charter, ministers were appointed and survived because they could command a majority in the Chamber rather than because they were the king's choice. The balance of power had slipped effectively to parliament.

Charles X was unwilling to accept this situation. He came to the throne with a record that was hardly likely to reassure the heirs to the revolutionary and Napoleonic tradition. The first of the émigrés, the essence of everything that Coblenz had stood for, involved in, or suspected of complicity in, every plot against Revolution or Empire, known for his coolness towards the Charter and his clumsy handling of the sensitivities of Napoleonic officials and soldiers in 1814, the leading figure in the network of agents known as the 'occult' government, directed from his apartments in the Pavillon de Marsan, the new king seemed to personify the spirit of the *ancien régime* and Counter-Revolution, the 'crowned head of the ultras'. Some of this had, of course, applied to Louis XVIII: 'an old émigré, the old relic of the ideas and manners of Versailles', Rémusat had described him in the passage quoted above. Yet these characteristics were largely confined by the old king to a harmless obsession with the trivialities of court etiquette. In the case of Charles his accession was loudly acclaimed by the ultras as the coming triumph of Counter-Revolution: 'The throne is occupied by an émigré', declared 'Le Drapeau Blanc' in January 1825, 'one of those princes who from exile addressed to their faithful servants those calls to which they have responded so nobly. . . .' That alone was enough to disturb a political system where suspicion between the two traditions was a permanent feature of the scene.

The charges and counter-charges, the dramatic language, especially of the ultra press, make a clear judgement as to Charles' intentions difficult. In particular accusations of Counter-Revolution had been made so often and included such a wide range of people ever since the start of the Revolution itself as to lose any precision. There were not many individuals and groups who at some stage had not been accused of being counter-revolutionaries, and the finding of plots, real or imaginary, was part of the common coin of the whole period. There was no difficulty in adding Charles' policies and suspected activities to the formidable list and seeing his reign as a single conspiracy to overthrow the Charter. It was, of course, no great secret that he had not approved of the details of the Charter, any more than many of the ultras. That did not, however, mean a wish to overturn it and restore the absolutism of the *ancien régime*. No one with even a modest degree of political realism thought that it was possible to turn back the clock: the world of 23 June and Coblenz was dead at least in its details even if broad principles remained alive. Charles not only had just enough political sense to understand this, but a denial of a constitution was also contrary to the principles on which he and his remaining ultra friends had acted since 1787. Charles prided himself on his consistency although it would be better described as a stubborn inflexibility and failure to learn from experience: 'Two men have not changed since 1789: Lafayette and myself', he said. It was not something particularly to be proud of but it does provide a guide to his attitude – it would probably be an error to call it his thinking.

He undoubtedly therefore believed in a form of constitutional monarchy. It was a fundamental belief of the aristocratic and princes' Counter-Revolution that the old monarchy was constitutional but that this constitution had been subverted by Louis XIV. The Charter of 1814 on this analysis was, again to quote 'Le Drapeau Blanc', 'merely an extension to the laws of the monarchy. . . . They are new liberties added to the ancient national rights.' The restored monarchy was thus, as an ultra claimed, no more constitutional than it had always been. The key point was the nature of this constitution and the distribution of power within it. This, together with the interpretation of the significance of the Charter, was one of the many points where the two worlds of Revolution and Counter-Revolution drew apart as they had been doing from fairly similar premises since 1787. Charles saw the balance within the constitution as resting decisively with the Crown, while the Assembly acted in a representative and advisory capacity, a support rather than a check. It was in this sense among others that elements of the 23 June programme, in principle but not in detail, can be found surviving into the Restoration. The Charter had clearly developed in a quite different direction since 1814 and needed correction. That was all the more necessary because of the behaviour of an opposition which Charles considered not merely factious but disloyal and revolutionary. Behind the liberal, on this thinking, stood the men of 1789 but they needed dealing with in a way from which Louis XVI, to his cost and that of the throne, had flinched. There had to be firmness, the need to get on one's horse and draw the sword of defiance.

How this was to be achieved was another matter altogether. If Charles and his circle probably had a general idea of what they wanted, they had little clear idea of how to achieve it. Partly this has to be put down to an absence of much political sense or understanding of the world, let alone sympathy with it, produced by the Revolution. In this, as in so much else, Charles had, unlike Louis XVIII, changed little:

he remained the man of Coblenz and Holyrood and all the other points of the emigration wanderings. There was an essential frivolity about him which justifies the contemporary description: 'mature years without maturity'. Neither, after the departure of Villèle, were there advisers who could correct his superficial grasp of affairs or correct his erratic approach to policy-making. Yet there was no consensus among ultras either, no unified base from which Charles could launch a determined effort to revise the constitution. The very size and apparent security afforded by the ultra majority in the *Chambre Retrouvée* of 1824 enabled the ultras to break up into an aimless factionalism in which good government and responsible opposition were forgotten in the search for power, or the scoring of points. This fragmentation of the ultras was only to be made worse by government policies. In the end more serious, however, was the deepening division within the propertied class as a whole, that is the notable class which had emerged from the Revolution. In social and economic terms there was little to distinguish the elements of this group: wealthy, conservative, cultivated, far from revolutionary, concerned above all with the maintenance of social order. Yet the gulf between the traditions of Revolution and Counter-Revolution was enormous: they were two worlds which could only be linked by a constant effort of reassurance by government. Charles X was quite unable even to begin to understand this society to which he had returned in 1814.

It was not a fault possessed by the minister he inherited. Villèle held office for longer than any other restoration minister and was probably the ablest of them all, setting a permanent mark on French financial administration. He was an ultra who had come to terms with political realities – not as rare a bird as might be thought. He had been mayor of Toulouse in the first stages of the restoration, an early member of the *Chevaliers de la foi* and also the author of a pamphlet explaining why the Crown should not be restrained by a Charter. He had therefore been the great hope of the *Chevaliers* and had the confidence of the comte d'Artois. Both were to be lost, although in Charles' case more slowly and reluctantly. The shift in Villèle's attitude was the consequence of policies which flowed naturally from his background and character. He had, says his biographer Fourcassié, along with a peasant sense of realism, a distaste for the romantic outpourings of the age and the posturings of some of its figures. Every day's diary entry started with a note on the weather. His deepest commitment was to the land and his conviction that in it lay the foundations of the social order. Politics had to give way before this inescapable fact. In that sense as in much else his values were those of the ultra. He remained, in Guizot's opinion, 'at heart a man of the *ancien régime*'. But his unflamboyant, dull style, practical approach, willingness to adjust to opinion, were unlikely to endear him to the wilder shores of ultra thought, while his policies alarmed the liberals. Even so, he managed to stay in office for almost seven years, a considerable achievement by the standards of any nineteenth-century system of constitutional government. This was largely due to his skill in managing the Chamber; but it also had something to do with his clear idea of what he wanted to achieve and the method of achieving it. His object was to end the gulf between the two traditions in French society, to bring together the parts of the notable élite behind sound government: 'I was born to end revolution', he claimed.

The basis of this would not be widely different from what most ultras wanted: the creation of a strong, politically responsible, well-established landed aristocracy of the type to be found in England. This was not an unreasonable aim: the notables, of whatever tradition, were overwhelmingly landed just as the economy of France was agricultural and pre-industrial. In the end, however, the price of various concessions to ultra opinion was to alarm the liberals without satisfying the ultras, reopen old wounds and raise old battle cries, and to turn a fairly scattered and unformulated opposition, only a fragment of which was unsympathetic to the Bourbons, into a more numerous and organised movement. Once Villèle, increasingly isolated in the Chamber, had gone, the bad political sense of Charles and Polignac turned this movement into opposition to the dynasty itself. That, however, was after some years of mounting anxiety and still needed almost unbelievable political ineptitude to turn into a Revolution. The accession of Charles X was not, therefore, the start of a slide into inevitable disaster except in so far as his inflexibility and incompetence made such an outcome likely once the restraining hand of ministers like Villèle had been removed.

The area in which most anxiety was aroused was religious policy. Some misgivings had already been stirred up by the appointment of a bishop Frayssinous in 1822 as the head of the Université, the authority which controlled the education system, but this was no serious threat except to those who wanted to see one. This was indeed the case with the whole of the religious policy of the 1820s: there never was a danger of a clerical 'take-over'. It was rumour and suspicion, feeding on other sources of disquiet, which promoted the belief in an occult power whose tentacles spread through every branch of administration, a secret web of intrigue and influence known as the Congregation placing its members in positions of power and influence. This belief, based on a mix of fact and fiction, misunderstanding and confusion, nevertheless had a deep appeal and entered into common tradition. Balzac's *Le curé de Tours*, about the destruction of a provincial priest at the hands of secret enemies, represents (in the 1830s) the continuing assumption that such a network had existed. At a popular level it was a matter of belief in a 'priest party' or simply the all-pervading power of the Jesuits. Even Charles himself was occasionally rumoured to have taken Holy Orders, a glimpse of purple in his dress being enough to fuel such gossip. There is no doubting his commitment to the Church but a clerical policy in the sense of giving the clergy equal authority, as opposed to allowing it that scope to 'moralise' the nation which it had always looked for, was out of the question. The real nature of the religious policies of the government was less important than the suspicions which emerged in a charged atmosphere where cries of Counter-Revolution and Revolution were easily raised.

The coronation in 1825 raised the first of such suspicions. Although some urged that a coronation was unnecessary and out-of-place in the circumstances of Restoration France, a ceremony of some sort was not inappropriate or outrageous. It was, of course, a perfectly normal aspect of a monarchical system. Louis XVIII had not been crowned simply because of the unusual conditions of 1814–15 and the state of his health. The contentious point of the 1825 coronation was less its fact than its style, its theatrical and ludicrous echoes of old France and above all its overwhelmingly religious atmosphere and trappings. This again may be overstressed – all coronations are religious ceremonies. In 1825 it was a feature taken to the point of absurdity, having not just an antique and superstitious element but the unedifying sight of the king prostrating himself before the archbishop of Reims. It was the starting point for the lampoons and satirical verses, particularly those of Béranger.

More serious was the Law on Sacrilege in the same year. It was a law, making offences against devotional objects in Catholic churches a capital offence, which deeply divided even the ultras. It was a measure which the government itself had withdrawn only a few months previously and over which Villèle had strong misgivings – it went against all his instincts. In fact it was part of his efforts to secure the support of the *Chevaliers de la foi*, a substantial body in the Chamber after 1824, who could feel a sense of betrayal at Villèle's failure to follow through their programme. What the programme was, Bertier outlined in a note to a provincial *bannière*, or group, of the *Chevaliers*: it included compensation for the émigrés and the families of those whose property had been confiscated; an increase in the authority of the fathers of families; administrative decentralisation, to which he later added the restoration of the old provinces; the right of the king to nominate to all military ranks; press censorship; laws against sacrilege; precedence for religious over civil marriage. Some elements of this were not distasteful to Villèle, for example compensation to the émigrés; but as a package it was politically unacceptable even to large numbers of ultras. The religious content was especially so, and Bertier's speech on the Sacrilege Bill (quoted in Chapter 5) urging in inflated language the necessity for kings to defend the cause of religion if their thrones were to be safe, came in for much ridicule. Villèle had, in fact, removed Bertier from the Council of State in August 1824.

The Sacrilege Bill was therefore a political device, never enforced and probably unenforceable. It nevertheless had a considerable effect on the future of the Restoration. It divided the ultras, many of them detecting in it the influence of the ultramontanes, that is the section within the Church which emphasised the authority of the Papacy. Ultracism may have stood for a society with a clear religious, Catholic, dimension but not for handing over the State to the Church. This was never, anyway, the intention of the *Chevaliers*. Such a view is nowhere to be found in Bertier's passionate speech on the Bill. In spite of this it was easy to promote the idea of a clerical conspiracy – why otherwise should the government have reintroduced a measure it had only recently withdrawn? The belief in a mysterious network of clericals was given wider currency by the immensely popular 'Memoire à consulter sur en système religieux et politique, tendant à renverser la religion, la société et le trône ('Guide to a religious and political system leading to the overthrow of religion, society and the throne') by the comte de Montlosier, an ultra and former émigré, but Gallican in his religious views. He claimed that nearly 48,000 members belonged to the Congregation. The accuracy of this matters less than the belief, now widespread, in a 'priest party'. It was a belief which disturbed the ultras to the point where, Broglie thought, the debates on the Sacrilege Bill marked the decline of a king's party in the Chamber.

The religious question was therefore a virtually inescapable source of misunderstanding which rallied liberal opinion and divided the ultras. Opposition to the government, if not to the dynasty, cut across any simple social analysis and included old nobility and émigrés as well as heirs to the revolutionary tradition. This division within the same fairly narrow class, a division between two traditions, was itself becoming blurred as cross-splits occurred in the 1820s.

This increasing tendency towards the blurring of divisions is to be found in another of Villèle's measures: the compensation in 1825 to the émigrés for the loss of their lands. It was a measure which had a lot to be said in its favour since it removed the uncertainty surrounding the lands acquired during the Revolution. It also fitted Villèle's policy of creating a unified landed class as the base for a secure monarchy. It could well have had the effect of eliminating at least one of the sources of division within the notable class. The result was the opposite of what was intended. Not only was the property-owning class riddled with resentment at the means of financing the operation out of the bonds, which affected the bourgeoisie above all, but the compensation left the émigrés themselves resentful at the levels of compensation and the choice of who benefited.

It also reopened the old grievances against the émigrés as a class: not, as they saw themselves, people who had suffered for their loyalties and principles, but as traitors to their country, taking up arms against it at a critical point of its history. The indemnity angered the business and investing classes who held *rentes* but it also increased the already considerable irritation of all those humbler individuals whose sacrifices for the Counter-Revolution had been as great in personal if not in material terms as those of the more eminent figures who were now given large sums. The West secured what amounted to a mere 50 francs a head compared, for example, to a duc de Fitzjames or de la Tremoille who got 289,000 francs. The image of the émigré as a figure enriching himself at the expense of the country he had betrayed was enhanced. It was, said a contemporary, 'a plaster applied to still unclosed scars, several of which were reopened by the remedy itself'. In the Côte d'Or, where only 42 communes were indemnified compared to 200 aristocrats, a local newspaper ironically commented: 'The great banquet prepared by the men who were to occupy the principal places is over and France, which has met the expenses, will not be annoyed to learn of the satiated guests it has so graciously entertained.'

The Sacrilege Law, the coronation, the indemnity to the émigrés gave impetus therefore to the unease which was never far below the surface of

Restoration politics. Above all, the notables in the Revolutionary tradition needed that reassurance which Charles' government was clearly unable to provide. Instead, its politics and attitudes amounted to a rejection of the relationship between the institutions of government and the values of that society whose roots lay in 1789. As the government wandered from one contentious measure to another every move could be seen as yet one more piece of evidence of a plot and every government defeat another triumph over Counter-Revolution. Thus a Bill to restore a limited right of primogeniture in 1826 was fought as a battle between the France of the Revolution and the France of the *ancien régime* in which the supporters of the Bill argued for the superior merits of land over finance. 'The owners of the soil', said Peyronnet, 'have a country, capitalists have not.' It was to be a familiar argument throughout the century, and not just in France. The distinction had no real social meaning, however, except in terms of the values of two traditions and even that could be unclear. The diminishing circle of ultras around Charles were, in short, steadily contracting their base within the ranks of property. It was a policy pursued through to the end. By 1827 Villèle himself was isolated between a strengthened liberal wing organised for electoral purposes by the society *Aide-toi, le Ciel t'aidera* (Heaven helps those who help themselves), and to his Right a fragmented ultra wing. The unpopularity of the ministry was extending to Charles himself as his hostile reception by the Paris National Guard in 1827 demonstrated. The resulting disbandment of the Guard did nothing to help promote the king's popularity although he remained convinced, in the royal tradition, that Paris was an unrepresentative hothouse of political dissent and that in the provinces he and the monarchy were as popular as ever. His isolation within a small circle of like-minded intimates, many of whom had shared his experiences in exile, prevented a clear view of political realities.

By the end of 1827 Villèle's position had become so precarious in the Chamber that elections were called, which he had every expectation of winning. The results indicated the extent to which his policies had rallied an opposition which in 1824 had been tiny. Moderate royalists were returned in large numbers after a campaign fought largely as a defence of a threatened Charter. Villèle's resignation in January 1828 brought in Martignac as the head of a new ministry, widely regarded as offering an olive branch to liberal opinion. Yet in the end it produced no fresh way forward, mainly because Charles had no confidence in or liking for it; it was a stop-gap before a more acceptable government could be found. The king's intention was shown by his premature summons of Polignac from his London embassy in January 1829 to plan a new ministry. The measures passed by Martignac as a concession to liberal anxieties, for example a relaxation of the press laws, liberalisation of voting procedures, had no secure base, while clerical opposition to controls on the Jesuits and above all to the regulation of ecclesiastical schools caused division in the Church and did little to soothe the fears of those who saw conspiracy around every corner. The defeat of a Bill on the reorganisation of local government in April 1829 gave the king the opportunity to dissolve the ministry. In August he at last appointed his old friend Polignac as head of a new government in an atmosphere which by this time was heavy with intrigue.

The appointment of the Polignac ministry, including Bourmont, regarded as the man who had betrayed Napoleon on the eve of Waterloo, as well as being a former chouan leader, and Bourdonnaye, notorious for his hot-headed ultra pronouncements, was seen as a challenge to the constitution, a precursor of Counter-Revolution. 'So, Charles X remains the comte d'Artois of 1789', said Royer-Collard. It looked, thought Guizot, as if the flag of Counter-Revolution was to be raised over the Tuileries. The Right indeed saw it as a sign that battle was at least to be joined between royalism and Revolution.

Yet what did this mean in practical terms? There was a great deal of windy talk during the Restoration, charges and counter-charges, about Revolution and Counter-Revolution, at almost every point of political disagreement. Suspicion lurked around every corner. The expressions had long degenerated into all-purpose terms of abuse devoid of much precise meaning. If by 'Counter-Revolution' was meant a desire to turn the clock back to 1789 then hardly anyone thought this possible or desirable. In that sense at least Royer-Collard was wrong: Charles was not a man of 1789. The issue was not the constitution itself, which all shades other than the most extreme Right accepted, but the nature of the constitution and the society it should reflect and sustain. Here there was no agreement even among the ultras. There never had been. Accusations of Counter-Revolution, the term 'émigré', easily promoted the concept of a single anti-revolutionary bloc. That was a long way from the truth. The Counter-Revolution and the emigration had always been as diverse as the Revolution itself: the range of opinion on the Charter stretched from a minority who rejected it outright, to the abbé de Montesquiou who, in Guizot's words, realised the *ancien régime* was dead but would have liked to see 'it revived and rejuvenated by the new society', to Chateaubriand who regarded the Charter as the bridge between two worlds. Polignac, the apparent standard-bearer of reaction, certainly had no intention of revoking the Charter. He shared with Charles a lack of understanding and sympathy for the post-revolutionary world and little political sense, although he was not, in spite of much contemporary, and later, opinion, a fool. He admired the English system of constitutional government, and understood it enough to realise that it was not transferable to France because of the wholly different historical development of the two nations. His ideal was probably a medieval form of monarchical government based on a unified faith and chivalric aristocracy. These sorts of fancies were unique neither to Polignac nor to France: Young England was to toy with them in the 1830s and 1840s. He was, however, realistic enough to understand that it was out of the question.

The aim, more realistically, bore some resemblance to Villèle's as well as that of a number of the less extreme ultras: the reaffirmation of the central role of the Crown in the constitution, a parliament reflecting an influential aristocracy, both old and new, a stronger Chamber of Peers. In short, the regime would be, as Charles considered the Charter intended, constitutional but with the balance clearly in favour of the Crown. That balance would now be restored. The moment, as Charles saw it, was decisive in the same way that 1789 had been when, if Louis XVI had acted with firmness, the Crown could have been saved. Once again, revolutionaries in the guise of liberals and backed by an irresponsible press threatened the established order; and once again it was the duty of the king to defend and to hand on the monarchy in the form in which he had received it. What Charles and Polignac therefore had in mind was an irreversible shift of power in the direction of the monarchy and a revision of the electoral law so as to provide the support of a two-chamber parliament weighted in the favour of the wealthier landed magnates, whatever the source of that land.

How far that constituted Counter-Revolution in any sense other than the generalised all-purpose term of abuse it had largely become, is another matter. The elements of continuity with 1789 are thin but they do exist. The view of the Crown as a family affair is one. More important is the concept of the nature of the constitution as one in which a paternal and wise monarchy would be unhindered by the pretensions of an elected Chamber whose function, although essential, would be much as that envisaged for the Estates General of 1789: advisory and fiscal, a support but not an equal. The old constitution, in short, brought up to date but not superseded.

In almost all other respects, however, Counter-Revolution meant something quite different from what it had meant in 1789 and for much of the emigration. Charles and Polignac were so far from considering that they represented Counter-Revolution that they offered posts in the cabinet to moderate royalists. In part this reflects an absence of clear ideas in 1829, and in part their lack of understanding of political opinion; but it also indicates their belief in the constitutional correctness of their behaviour. There was never any question of overturning the administrative and judicial structure of the Revolution and Empire and restoring the institutions of the old provinces, something to which many ultras retained a strong attachment. This was one of those many dilemmas which ultras found it impossible to resolve, as the rejection of Martignac's measure had revealed. The Right, in practice, always feared the consequences to royal authority of the possible decentralisation of power. Neither was the revolutionary social structure to be overturned except in the important respect that power would be more securely vested in the landed class. However, this was less important than it might appear because this class was itself the amalgam of the two traditions and upper-class society, like French society as a whole, was overwhelmingly landed. Most deputies, as was to be expected in a rural nation, were from the landed classes. In that sense the Revolution was under no threat. Yet it was perceived as such by the liberals, who were a conservative and cautious, not a revolutionary class, and were certainly not anxious to manufacture a threat where none existed. Lacking in definition though the term 'Counter-Revolution' may be, contemporaries probably had a reasonably accurate idea of what it meant. Their anxieties could undoubtedly have been pacified even at a late stage of the crisis by appropriate concessions and some tact. They came to fear the worst in part because of the course of the reign, but also because of the absence of any clear statement from the ministry. As the months passed a sense of conspiracy, always easy to develop, unfolded, and was not diminished by the hotheaded pronouncements of the ultras and their press.

In the end, however, even that was less important than the more fundamental lack of understanding by the king and ministry of what the constitution was really about. In Guizot's words, Polignac 'believed

[it] was reconcilable with the political preponderance of the old nobility and the final supremacy of the old royalty, and he persuaded himself that the new institutions could be developed by allowing them to serve the domination of the influences that they had been formed precisely to abolish or control'. The issue was more than the enhancement of the power of the Crown within the constitution, although that was important enough; it was the preponderance of the values of that part of the notable elite which derived its origins from pre-revolutionary France. That social group did not have to be the old nobility or former émigrés, any more than the liberals were necessarily men of business or the law, even if many were. It was attitudes of mind which, in the end, distinguished the two sides. The ministry, and Charles, had no understanding of the post-revolutionary mind. They rejected the principles on which political life had been based since the Revolution in favour of a return, if not to a mythical 'golden age', at least to a relationship between Crown and governed which had vanished in 1789. In that sense, paradoxically, the Right had become revolutionaries seeking to overturn the established order. It was a role they continued to play for the next century and more. Counter-Revolution in these forms therefore represented disorder and upheaval while the liberals stood for the defence of the status quo: they were the true conservatives.

How were the changes to be carried out? Polignac and Charles were sensitive to any charges of wishing to act unconstitutionally. This was one reason why nothing was done during the autumn and winter, quite apart from lack of ideas. In the meantime elements in the liberals were talking of a French 1688 although without much general support. The crisis began in March 1830 with the reopening of the Chamber and the king's address. It made vague threats against unnamed forces said to be challenging the rights of the throne. The reply from the Chamber of Deputies, approved by 221 to 181, questioned this and the royal conception of the constitution, as well as declaring their lack of confidence in the ministry. The issue was not, therefore, the constitution, or the dynasty, even if some were beginning to suggest alternatives, but the question of the balance of power within the constitution and, underlying that, alternative views of the nature of France itself. The deadlock might have been broken by a change of ministry or even the announcement of a moderate ministerial programme to allay fears and win over a majority among the 221. The narrowness alone of this majority shows how anxious much of the Chamber was to avoid disorder and how easily the whole crisis could have been avoided. Instead the king chose to dissolve the Chamber and pour every effort into securing a favourable majority in the next one. It was during these weeks between March and June, when the elections were held, that more pronounced opposition to the dynasty itself surfaced and a virtually defunct republicanism also showed signs of life. The tactics of the ministry only made matters worse, for example the use of the Church as a channel of pressure and propaganda and the personal intervention of the king in the campaign.

The result, the return of almost all the 221, was a clear defeat for the ministry but not a rejection of the dynasty. That occurred because the king now chose to invoke Article XIV of the Charter, allowing him to take exceptional powers in a crisis. After much agonising in the cabinet, the consequence was the promulgation of four Ordinances on 26 July. Three of the Ordinances dealt with restrictions on the press, dissolution of the Chamber and the arrangements for the next elections and the meeting of the new Chamber. The central Ordinance was the third, which dealt with the franchise, the electoral system and the size of the Chamber. This represented the heart of whatever passed for Counter-Revolution. The structure of the Chamber was to be changed by reducing the number of deputies and renewing the membership annually by one-fifth; there was to be a five-year instead of a seven-year parliament; and the tax qualification for deputies and voters was to be raised as well as, crucially, computing the tax on land and personal property alone. Other taxes were not to be counted. In this way the business community, identified with the liberal vote, would be partially excluded. In practice the consequences may have been neither as drastic as the opposition thought nor as effective as the government hoped. Other measures for the procedures at elections were designed to reinforce the preponderance of land and official pressure. This may also not have worked had it ever been implemented. If the object of the changes was flawed at the technical level, and so unlikely to produce the anticipated results, there were far more important and fundamental reasons why they were likely to fail.

The whole thrust of the Ordinances was in the wrong direction even from the standpoint of what might have been in the interests of the Crown itself. The base of royal support was to be further narrowed down and control was to be centralised. This was not just to court disaster but also to reverse some of the traditional features of royal policy. Decentralisation had been a constant part of counter-revolutionary, and then ultra, policy which had been as constantly avoided in practice. Another aspect of the Counter-Revolution was, of course, its popular base. Ultra policy might have succeeded by making a bid for an alliance with popular royalism against an exploiting bourgeoisie either of law or business or land. The two policies were linked and the rejection of both was for much the same reasons; that rejection was a key factor in the isolation of Bourbon royalism which in the end contributed to its downfall although the ineptitude of the king and his ministers must occupy the chief place.

Popular royalism had been a constant feature of the Revolution, of the closing years of the Empire, and of the Restoration itself. Aristocratic Counter-Revolution had attempted to forge links with it during the Revolution and to sustain its memories, mainly in the West, during the Restoration. The duchesses of Berry and Angoulême made tours in the West as part of a deliberate effort to cultivate the Vendéan legend, an effort supported by landowners who through festivals and commemorations also kept alive old memories and, more importantly, a 'special relationship' between nobility and peasantry. The purpose was deliberately, as Petitfrère argues, to promote popular cohesion 'around the régime's twin pillars of Church and aristocracy'. Mme de la Rochejacquelein's memoirs, written for her by Barante in 1816, laid the basis of the enduring myth of the idyllic 'golden age' of the pre-revolutionary Vendée in which aristocracy and people had lived in rustic harmony. Another widow of a Vendéan leader, Mme de Bonchamps, lent support to this in her memoirs as well. The aristocratic emphasis on the rights of the provinces and their customs could reinforce their claims to be the friends of popular liberties against the uniformity imposed from outside by urban, especially Parisian and, from the viewpoint of the Midi, northern influences.

This existing pattern was strengthened by another feature of royalism, social catholicism. This also was not new. An element in Catholic royalism's conflict with Protestantism in the Gard, as we have seen, had been its claim to represent a more caring, less exploitative, relationship with textile workers than the urban merchants. It was given added point by the developing industries of departments such as the Nord and could fit easily into the distaste, social as well as traditional, of landed wealth for 'new' money, especially of the mobile variety. The ultramontane Lamennais was already developing that defence of the rights of the poor and the obligations of society towards them that was eventually to take him on to the popular side in 1848. Bonald also, the theorist of monarchical absolutism, could produce a defence of a society which acted as the protector of the individual against a rapacious capitalism. It was a conclusion which followed naturally from a rejection of the individualistic view of society. An alliance with popular royalism could therefore be defended not as an opportunistic, even cynical, political device but as entirely in accordance with tradition, theory and practice. A policy of widening the franchise in order to overwhelm the liberal opposition was urged by some ultras as practical politics. The July Ordinances instead went along the worst possible route: they not only rejected the possibility of a popular alliance but also split the notable class which, united, would have rescued the monarchy as it did, for a time, under Louis Philippe. The reason for such a decision could simply be allowed to rest with the misjudgement of Charles and Polignac. Those personal failings were, however, reinforced by the position of the ultras. They were caught in a thicket of insoluble dilemmas.

The policies of decentralisation, of support for the customary rights of communities and provinces, of sympathy towards 'folklorique' practices and paternalistic concern for the social condition of workers in developing factory industries, all involved the question of the relationship between central government and the landed elite on the one hand, and the populace on the other. How was control to be exercised over potentially unruly subjects? The ideal was of a deferential and grateful people looking to their natural leaders for guidance and protection. This did not work. Instead the people showed a disturbing tendency to get out of hand. The uneasy relationship between aristocratic leadership and popular Counter-Revolution had frequently demonstrated the gulf between the two. Popular Counter-Revolution had its own roots and its own objectives and the alliance between the two wings was often one of mutual convenience rather than affection. The leadership of the aristocracy was accepted, or demanded, on terms which were barely approved or sometimes rejected by potential leaders. Deep misunderstandings were frequent. Popular royalism was therefore harnessed to the Bourbon cause at the latter's peril as the events of 1814–15 in the South showed. It was not easy to put the cork back in the bottle once the genie of popular disorder was out. In the West the channelling of local patriotism into royalist forms had some greater success but even here there were limits to active support. The duchesse de Berry misjudged the enthusiasm of her reception in 1828 and found its limits four years later when she attempted, and failed, to raise the Vendée once again. Behind so many of the traditional, folklorique, practices of local life were elements, also, which challenged authority and undermined the very social control and cohesion which the elites sought to impose. The same uncertain attitude could be found in social Catholicism where sympathy towards working conditions stopped short at condoning independent acts of insubordination by the workers in the form of strikes. They were energetically put down. The problem, therefore, was how to defend the rights of communities and popular traditions within the framework of an orderly and hierarchical society where the paternalistic regard of landowner and employer would be met with proper gratitude but not spill over into unruly behaviour. It was a problem beyond the capacity of ultra notables to solve because it could not be solved within their terms of reference.

It was a problem which the devolution of power through decentralisation could only increase. In the end the ultra attachment to the old provinces remained a matter of sentiment rather than action for much the same reasons as the attachment to the rights of 'the people': it led to loss of control. In fact, as Angoulême made plain in 1815 when there had been talk of a 'Kingdom of the Midi', there was no question of reversing the centralised structure of the state. Such a policy would not only have abandoned one of the most valuable legacies of the Revolution towards which the Crown and its administrators had been aiming in the course of the *ancien régime*: it would also have delivered much of France over to the disorderly local control of the sort of elements which had only just been brought to heel in the Gard; or elsewhere more radical, even republican, interests might take over. Local notables could not always be trusted to exercise the right degree of authority or even be able to do so.

The dilemma which crippled the style of ultra politics as represented by the circle around Charles and Polignac went therefore to the heart of counter-revolutionary politics itself. It could only succeed by broadening its base and establishing an alliance with popular royalism on the basis of respect for local aspirations, social welfare, protection of customary practices. But this ran counter to the paternalism, hierarchical concepts and Bourbon centralism which resisted the challenge any such programme would have presented to social and political control. The alternative was to make an alliance with the upper bourgeoisie, to cement the links between all forms of wealth of whatever source and place it behind a monarchy which accepted full partnership with a parliamentary system in which the balance was tilted in favour of an Assembly. That was to be the solution adopted by the Orléans monarchy, just as it had been by this time in England. For the ultras it was out of the question because it would have meant accepting the values associated with the Revolution. In some respects Revolution and Counter-Revolution stood for similar principles such as the defence of order and property, civil liberties and constitutional checks on power. It was the ultra-dominated Assembly of 1815–16 which established the claims of the Assembly against the Crown and government, and Villèle rested his long period in office on his parliamentary skill. It was the bases of this which differed; for the ultra individual freedom was inseparable from the group such as the Church or the family, and any change must be sanctioned by traditional forms, a reinterpretation of the past rather than a break with it. The Revolution, from the ultra's viewpoint, was just such a break and the result was to fragment society to a collection of competing materialistic individuals and the state a mere temporary convenience, with no moral base, to be altered at the fancy of whatever fleeting group holds power. The Bourbons were not just trying to turn the clock back in the social sense of reconstituting the dominant group of 1789, but in trying to assert a set of values which were the opposite of what the Revolution had created. It was in that sense that 1830 was a failed counter-revolutionary coup. The monarchy had become isolated from the post-revolutionary world and even within the ranks of many of its natural supporters. The army for the last time in the century acted politically and abandoned a regime towards which it had become indifferent. But the regime had itself abandoned the new France.

The July Monarchy which replaced it hardly seems to differ. Some historians have questioned whether the word Revolution is appropriate for 1830. On the other hand 1830 saw a massive change in the administrative personnel of France especially of the prefectoral body, most of whom resigned or were dismissed. Some returned later, just as some Legitimists were to find it possible to rally to Orléanism. There were a few plots in the 1830s, most notably the duchesse de Berry's attempt to provoke a western rising. In the end most Legitimists retired to their estates and consolidated their local power, often with some success. Others, as for example in Toulouse, remained, in Higgs' description, a diminishing band of social fossils adhering to out-of-date ideas. In 1830 the Revolution appeared to have won a decisive victory.

Conclusion

Lefebvre considered that the Revolution was not decisively won until 1830. Up to that point its achievements were uncertain and insecure. Much depends on what is understood by the Revolution. Lefebvre's interpretation was the victory of the 'notables' by which he meant principally the upper bourgeoisie. The Restoration excluded them from full participation in government but under the July Monarchy, which 'brought to power a prince who accepted the Revolution's principles' they now enjoyed its political fruits. Those who did so remained, of course, almost as restricted in numbers as under the Bourbon Restoration. There was a slight widening of the channels of advancement and, as a result, the social composition of court circles, and the upper reaches of administration, and politics. The notable class, in the sense not just of the upper bourgeoisie but of the rich and influential elements of French society, now established that dominance they were to enjoy for much of the century.

In that respect, however, 1830 was not a victory but a defeat for all those who saw the Revolution as standing for much more than the rights of property with full participation in society defined by wealth. Most of the political upheavals of the next hundred years have at their root the efforts of those who had been excluded to assert their claims to the legacy of the Revolution. What that legacy was could be widely interpreted, from the limited constitutional forms of 1789 to a social republic drawing on the inspiration of 1793. Nevertheless, some principles could be commonly accepted: the doctrine of natural rights, of the primacy of the individual over the state, parliamentary sovereignty, equality of access to office (limited by whatever qualifications may have been thought necessary) and social esteem, equality of rights before the law and liberty of conscience. Even some of these may have been contested, for example under the Second Empire. Yet Napoleon III also considered himself an heir of the revolutionary tradition even while being cool towards such a revolutionary principle as parliamentary sovereignty. He nevertheless rested his authority on popular sanction. In the end the revolutionary tradition may simply come down to just such a view of the basis of authority: that it was derived from periodically renewed expressions of variously defined popular approval, reinforced by certain propositions such as natural rights, and not from any moral or religious force drawn from traditions represented in institutions such as the Crown or the Church.

It was on those conflicting approaches to the nature of authority that the Revolution and Counter-Revolution took their respective stands. In that sense the Counter-Revolution survived any checks such as 1830 because it was as much a permanent part of the French and European political tradition as the Revolution itself. It drew on a body of thought and attitudes which were not to be extinguished by setbacks. If, therefore, French history in the nineteenth and early twentieth centuries is about the slow expansion of the revolutionary heritage, it is also about the opposition presented by the alternative, counter-revolutionary, heritage. The guardians of that inheritance were the Legitimists. In 1871, when there was a monarchist majority in the Assembly, much of it of the Legitimist variety, there was again the opportunity, as in 1830, of defeating the Revolution from a position of power. That collapsed with the failure of MacMahon's attempt in 1877 to sustain the majority. It was a battle which continued in various forms, with Legitimism becoming overshadowed by a new-style, more strident and populist Right, for the rest of the Third Republic, culminating under Vichy in a victory of sorts for Counter-Revolution. The real victory of the Revolution and the final defeat of Counter-Revolution was to come in 1944. The blood-letting of the liberation was the last and most costly in the long series of conflicts stretching back to 1789.

Counter-Revolution can easily seem at this distance one of those many lost historical causes, its supporters representing a politically unrealistic and socially backward class, intellectually cobwebbed and reactionary. This might well apply to some of its supporters; but any such description would fail to explain its enduring strength and appeal, the very real challenge which it presented to the alternative, the revolutionary, tradition. It was never simply a reactionary movement – indeed at no point did any except the incurable romantic wish to turn back the clock or seriously believe that was possible. It drew instead on arguments and impulses, on positive reasons, which exercised a powerful appeal to wide sections of the French people and Europe as a whole. The legacy of the Revolution was deeply divisive as well as, for many, a betrayal, constantly reaffirmed, of their hopes. The repeated emphasis on unity in nineteenth- and twentieth-century France is a reminder of its absence. The Revolution, while it unified France administratively divided it politically and even morally, at the same time appearing to promote the fragmentation of society into competing and materialistic individuals by its emphasis on wealth and property as the base of success and esteem. The counter-revolutionary Right offered a different focus for patriotic unity, one based on tradition, authority and a religious framework for society. At the centre there was, of course, the monarchy, rising above the conflicts of ephemeral parties and factions, the living symbol of the nation's history, the creator of its past greatness. Then there was the Catholic Church, of which France was 'the eldest daughter', again associated with the greatest periods of its history. Its function was more than a unifying one: its purpose was to moralise a secular, almost pagan, nation, to lift it above the pursuit of selfish gain. Counter-Revolution placed the individual within the group, that is the province, or the profession, or the town and village, and so on, each mutually supportive rather than destructively competitive and uncaring. The growth of social Catholicism, for example, was a natural outcome of such beliefs. They also indicate that the counter-revolutionary tradition cannot be dismissed merely as the sentimental attachment of antiquated groups to a lost cause. The emphasis on the land, always a feature of the propaganda and thought of the Right, as opposed to shallow and 'unhealthy' urban values fitted neatly into this structure.

Yet in the end it was the revolutionary tradition which had the most powerful appeal. Counter-Revolution was never short of individual leaders of talent, even genius. In many respects they were more admirable figures than their opponents: the Restoration period set standards for honest government, careful management of the finances, disinterested public service which no later French regime quite matched. But they were drawn from a limited circle heavily representative of the aristocracy; and even later in the century, Legitimism too often was associated with provincial noblemen whose interests and influence rested on rural paternalism. These people found not just a republic objectionable but republicans socially distasteful – indeed for some this was the real problem: inviting republicans to dinner was more difficult than conceding the republic, as one of them said during the early stages of the Third Republic. Legitimism was also unable, and usually unwilling, to distance itself from the Church, while the latter's efforts to break with monarchism only resulted in damaging splits. By the end of the century the counter-revolutionary tradition which drew its inspiration from old-style Legitimism was divided, even discredited, and in the process of being taken over and directed on different lines through such movements as *Action Française*. These movements were to be populist in a way that Legitimism had always failed to achieve.

If there was a central weakness to the Counter-Revolution it was its inability to join together the two parts, so to speak, of the aristocratic and popular wings. This failure was evident from the earliest stages. The émigré princes and much of their aristocratic circle rarely understood the nature and purpose of the popular insurrections of the Revolution, not altogether surprisingly since these had origins which were separate in motives and aim from those of the emigration. Ignorance promoted misunderstanding and even some distaste among many of those émigrés who returned to join the popular movements. The peasantry, at least in the West, were never the instruments of external manipulators, any more than they were of their own leaders. As often as not any alliance was one of mutual and temporary advantage. Even so, royalism put down deep roots in some areas of the country such as the West, where it became a distinguishing mark of regional identity, and in regions of the South. Yet Legitimism failed to turn this base into the reality of political power. It was the new Right, of the twentieth century, which attempted to do so, but in a style which was quite distinct from the traditional monarchists.

Legitimism saw its relationship with the populace in paternalistic terms. In effect it assumed a vanished 'golden age' based on landed society. This was the ideal to which government should aspire: 'the earth does not lie', said Pétain in 1940. It was unrealistic but anything else might open up the way to political equality, the realisation of individual social aspirations, the rejection of the tutelage of the traditional hierarchy: in short those very principles of the Revolution which the heirs of the Counter-Revolution rejected. The Republic, however, for all its shortcomings and disappointments, its narrow emphasis on property, its deep conservatism, its rejection of any measures which might upset its bourgeois base, was based on a hard realism and offered channels of advancement and improvement, the possibility of changing the status quo, to fresh levels of society, whether it was those who responded to Gambetta's appeal in the 1870s or to the working-class supporters of the Popular Front in the 1930s. Legitimism could never offer those opportunities. Neither could the populist Right, fascist or semi-fascist. It was only when the Republic had been swept away in defeat in 1940 that the latest form of the counter-revolutionary tradition, with its rejection of parliamentary sovereignty, its assertion of authority, its emphasis on the supposed enduring values of the land against those of the rootless town, was able briefly to take power. Its failure meant the end of Counter-Revolution.

Bibliography

Abbreviations

FHS	*French Historical Studies*
JMH	*Journal of Modern History*
HJ	*Historical Journal*
PP	*Past and Present*
Trans. RHS	Transactions of the Royal Historical Society

Beach, V. W., *Charles X of France* (Boulder, Colorado, 1971).

Behrens, C. B. A., *Society, Government and the Enlightenment: the Experience of 18th Century France and Prussia* (London, 1985).

Bertier, de Sauvigny, G., *The Bourbon Restoration*, tr. Lynn M. Case (Philadelphia, 1966).

Bien, D., 'The French Revolution Seen from the Right', *Transactions of the American Philosophical Soc.*, No. 46 (1956).

Bien, D., 'The Army in the French Enlightenment: Reform, Reaction and Revolution', *PP*, 85 (1979), 68–98.

Blanning, T. C. W., *The Origins of the French Revolutionary Wars* (London, 1986).

Blanning, T. C. W., *The French Revolution in Germany: Occupation and Resistance in the Rhineland 1792–1802* (Oxford, 1983).

Cobb, R., *Reactions to the French Revolution* (Oxford, 1972).

Crook, M. H., 'Federalism and the French Revolution: the Revolt of Toulon in 1793', *History*, 65 (1980).

Doyle, W., *The Oxford History of the French Revolution* (Oxford, 1989).

Doyle, W., 'The Parlements', in Baker, K. M., *The Political Culture of the Old Regime* (Oxford, 1987).

Edmonds, B., '"Federalism" and Urban Revolution in France', *JMH*, 55 (1983), 22–53.

Fitzpatrick, B., *Catholic Royalism in the Department of the Gard 1818–1852* (Cambridge, 1983).

Forrest, A., *Society and Politics in Revolutionary Bordeaux* (Oxford, 1975).

Fryer, W. R., *Republic or Restoration in France? 1794–7* (Manchester, 1965).

Godechot, J., *The Counter-Revolution: Doctrine and Action 1789–1804* (London, 1972).

Goodwin, A., 'Counter-Revolution in Brittany: the Royalist Conspiracy of the Marquis de la Rouerie 1791–1793', *Bull. of the John Rylands Library* (1957).

Greer, D., *The Incidence of the Emigration in the French Revolution* (Harvard, 1951).

Hampson, N., *Will and Circumstance: Montesquieu, Rousseau and the French Revolution* (London, 1983).

Hartman, M., 'The Sacrilege Law of 1825 in France: a study in anti-clericalism and myth-making', *JMH* (1972).

Hood, J. N., 'Protestant–Catholic Relations and the Roots of the First Popular Counter-Revolutionary Movement in France', *JMH*, 43 (June 1971).

Hood, J. N., 'Patterns of Popular Protest in the French Revolution: the Conceptual Contribution of the Gard', *JMH*, 48 (June 1976).

Hufton, O., 'The Seigneur and the Rural Community in 18th Century France', *Trans. RHS*, xxix (1979), 21–39.

Hutt, M., *Chouannerie and Counter-Revolution* (2 vols) (Cambridge, 1983).

Johnson, H. C., *The Midi in Revolution 1789–1793* (Princeton, 1986).

Jones, P. M., *The Peasantry in the French Revolution* (Cambridge, 1988).

Kossmann, E. H., *The Low Countries 1780–1940* (Oxford, 1978).

Lefebvre, G., *The French Revolution*, 2 vols (London, 1962).

Le Goff, T. J. A., *Vannes and its Region: a Study of Town and Country in 18th Century France* (Oxford, 1981).

Le Goff, T. J. A. and Sutherland, D. M. G., 'The Revolution and the Rural Community in 18th Century Brittany', *PP* (Feb. 1974).

Le Goff, T. J. A. and Sutherland, D. M. G., 'The Social Origins of Counter-Revolution in Western France', *PP*, 99 (May 1983).

Lewis, G., *The Second Vendée: the Continuity of Counter-Revolution in the Department of the Gard 1789–1815* (Oxford, 1978).

Lucas, C., *The Structure of the Terror: the Example of Javogues and the Loire* (Oxford, 1973).

Lucas, C., 'The Problem of the Midi in the French Revolution', *Trans. RHS*, xxviii (1978), 1–25.

Lucas, C. (ed.), *The French Revolution and the Creation of Modern Political Culture*, Vol. 2: *The Political Culture of the French Revolution* (Oxford, 1988).

Lyons, M., *The Revolution in Toulouse: an essay on Provincial Terrorism* (Durham, 1978).

MacManners, J., *The French Revolution and the Church* (London, 1969).

MacManners, J., *French Ecclesiastical Society under the Ancien Regime: a Study of Angers in the 18th Century* (Manchester, 1960).

Magraw, R., *France 1815–1914: the Bourgeois Century* (London, 1983).

Mansel, P., *Louis XVIII* (London, 1981).

Mitchell, H., 'The Vendée and Counter-Revolution: a Review Essay', *FHS*, v (1968), 405–29.

Mitchell, H., *The Underground War against Revolutionary France. The Missions of William Wickham 1794–1800* (Oxford, 1965).

Paret, P., *Internal War and Pacification. The Vendée 1789–1796* (Princeton, 1961).

Pilbeam, P., 'The Growth of Liberalism and the Crisis of the Bourbon Restoration 1827–1830', *HJ*, 25 (1982), 351–66.

Porch, D., *Army and Revolution: France 1815–1848* (London, 1974).
Richardson, N., *The French Prefectoral Corp 1814–1830* (Cambridge, 1966).
Schama, S., *Patriots and Liberators* (London, 1977).
Schama, S., *Citizens. A Chronicle of the French Revolution* (London, 1989).
Scott, W., *Terror and Repression in Revolutionary Marseilles* (London, 1973).
Sutherland, D. M. G., *The Chouans: the Social Origins of Popular Counter-Revolution in Upper Brittany 1770–1796* (Oxford, 1982).
Sutherland, D. M. G., *France 1789–1815: Revolution and Counter-Revolution* (London, 1985).
Tackett, T., *Priest and Parish: a Social and Political Study of the Curés in a Diocese of Dauphiné 1750–1791* (Princeton, 1977).
Tackett, T., 'The West in France in 1789: the Religious Factor in the Origins of the Counter-Revolution', *JMH*, 4 (1982), 715–45.
Tackett, T. and Langlois, C., 'Ecclesiastical Structures and Clerical Geography on the Eve of the French Revolution', *FHS*, xi (1980), 352–70.
Tackett, T., *Religion, Revolution and Regional Culture in 18th Century France: the Ecclesiastical Oath of 1791* (Princeton, 1986).
Tilly, C., *The Vendée* (Cambridge, Mass., 1964).
Weiner, M., *The French Exiles* (Westport, Conn., 1975).
Williams, W. H., 'Perspectives on the Parish Clergy on the Eve of the French Revolution', *Proceedings of the Fourth Annual Colloquium on Revolutionary Europe 1750–1850* (Gainsville, 1976).
Woolf, S., *A History of Italy 1700–1860* (London, 1979).
Wylie, L. (ed.), *Chanzeaux: A Village in Anjou* (Harvard, 1966).

Index